DEMOCRATS AND PROGRESSIVES

DEMOCRATS AND PROGRESSIVES

THE 1948 PRESIDENTIAL ELECTION AS A
TEST OF POSTWAR LIBERALISM

by *Allen Yarnell*

UNIVERSITY OF CALIFORNIA PRESS
BERKELEY   LOS ANGELES   LONDON
1974

University of California Press
Berkeley and Los Angeles, California

University of California Press, Ltd.
London, England

TO PAT

CONTENTS

Preface   ix

Acknowledgments   xiii

I.   Foreign Policy Splits Two Democrats   1

II.   1947: An Eventful Year   14

III.   Democratic Strategy: The Clifford Memorandum
       Analyzed   28

IV.   Reaction   46

V.   Issues of the Campaign   62

VI.   Liberals and 1948   87

VII.   End Results   108

Notes   115

Bibliography   137

Index   149

PREFACE

Third parties have played a prominent part in United States history since the mid-nineteenth century, and today names like Populist and Progressive are well known to all students of the American political experience. Among historians and political analysts, theories concerning third parties have long existed. John D. Hicks's classic study *The Populist Revolt*, published in 1931, first gave prominence to the theory that third parties influenced the major political parties.[1] In 1948 William B. Hesseltine wrote the following in support of Hicks's thesis: "Third parties have in the past made distinctive contributions to American politics and progressives can learn much from their history. In general, third parties have performed the function of calling attention to serious problems and pointing a way to their solution. They have stimulated—sometimes by frightening them—the lethargic or timid politicians of the major parties. They have advocated reforms which the older parties have adopted and enacted into law."[2] The 1948 Progressive party can be used to test this theory. Did Henry A. Wallace and his followers have a substantial impact on the Democrats?

The aim of the 1948 Progressive party was to redirect American foreign policy. In this respect the new party was quite different from other third party movements, for it was the first to attempt to focus on foreign rather than domestic policy. Through their presidential candidate, Henry A. Wallace (a former vice-president of the United States), the Progressives criticized U.S. actions, thus in the end causing their own downfall.

From the beginning, accusations were hurled alleging that the Progressive party was un-American and "soft on Communism." Further, citizens were asked to remember that the

Progressive party of 1948 had no roots in the past. The *Progressive* Magazine put it this way: "In a few months The Progressive will be 40 years old. In a few days Henry Wallace's 'Progressive' Party will be 40 days old. Despite the frenzied attempt of the Wallace strategists to claim common ancestry with The Progressive—by purporting to trace their genealogy back to Robert La Follette, Sr., the founder of this magazine—*there is no connection between us. None whatever.*" [3] In the same issue of the magazine, Professor Hesseltine was a bit more explicit in explaining why the Progressives had to be shunned: "it is perfectly clear to anyone who reads American history that the Cominformed Wallaceites have no moral right to the Progressive name. They are neither the physical nor the spiritual descendants of the Progressives of 1912 and 1924. They are not the breed of Teddy Roosevelt, old Bob La Follette, and George Norris." [4] Yet, there are those who maintain that the 1948 Progressives influenced the Democratic party in the campaign. Henry Wallace and the party's campaign manager C. B. (Beanie) Baldwin argued on November 4, 1948, that their party had been successful in that it had forced Harry Truman and the Democrats to campaign on the Progressive party's issues.[5] On November 13, Wallace, speaking to the National Committee of the Progressive party, told his audience, "the Democrats—as a result of our pressure—campaigned on a more forward looking program than ever before in [the] history of the Democratic Party." [6] And in 1952 after he had left the party, Wallace was still writing, "Although the PP cost Truman New York, I think on the whole we helped him through forcing him to adopt a program which won the election for him." [7] Former members of the now-defunct Progressive party like Beanie Baldwin and Len DeCaux still maintain that the party had an important impact.[8] This view is also held by Professor Karl Schmidt who has written of the 1948 Progressive party, that "For the first time in American history, the thunder of a party of discontent had been stolen, neither four nor forty years later, but in the very midst of the campaign." [9]

This interpretation has been challenged by former President Truman. In his memoirs he denies that the Wallace movement influenced his campaign, and he states that he fought against the "special interests" of the country as embodied in the Republican party and the Eightieth Congress. Truman claims that he "staked the race for the presidency on that one issue." [10] When he was asked in 1953 about the Progressive party's influence in the campaign, he responded by declaring that he did not think that it had had any. He further explained that he had not been pushed to the left because he had consistently taken positions in the "middle-of-the-road." [11]

Some commentators on the election disagree with the former chief executive about the impact of the Progressive party. In April 1949 former New Deal brain truster and Progressive party member Rexford Tugwell wrote that the Progressives had "forced President Truman far over to the left and so enabled him to win." In July 1971 Tugwell still held that the Progressives had forced a shift in the president's policies.[12] Tugwell, because of his Progressive affiliation, may have been biased in his judgment, but in 1959, historian David A. Shannon offered an assessment that was based, in part, on Tugwell's 1949 evaluation. Shannon argued that "Truman conducted a campaign designed to minimize the Wallace movement" and he "did move toward the Left during the campaign." [13] Jules Abels, who authored the first study of the entire election, also seems to believe that the Democrats moved left because of the Progressives. "The Truman program was designed to steal the thunder of Wallace's progressive platform with its appeal to New Dealers." [14] Abels held this view despite the fact that he had interviewed men like former Truman assistant Clark M. Clifford who denied its validity.

Karl Schmidt, who wrote the first full length account of the Wallace venture accepts the Tugwell view as does Curtis MacDougall in his three-volume account of the Progressive party.[15] Walter LaFeber joins Schmidt and MacDougall when he writes, "The Berlin blockade and Truman's shift to the left on domestic issues killed off any hopes that Progressives nursed of determining the election." [16] And in a recent extensive analysis of the 1948 election, Richard Kirkendall has concluded that the Wallaceites did pressure the president in terms of domestic campaign strategy.[17] The "shift theory," however, can be effectively countered by examining a strategy memorandum prepared by Clark Clifford in November 1947.

It is tempting to believe that in the United States a third party can have a positive effect on one or both of the major parties. This possibility adds flexibility to the party system and buttresses pluralist notions concerning the political process. Unfortunately, the thesis is untrue for 1948. The party of Henry Wallace did not force the Democrats to move left. In fact, the presence of the Progressives made it easier for the Truman forces to take tough stands on foreign policy issues thus aiding the Democrats in their 1948 presidential victory.

ACKNOWLEDGMENTS

In researching and writing this book, I was aided by a great number of people; they are too numerous to mention all by name. Specifically, however, I would like to thank Professors Otis Pease and Robert Burke of the University of Washington who gave of their time whenever I needed it. Professors Richard Kirkendall and Robert Griffith served as astute critics of papers delivered at professional meetings. The Harry S. Truman Library Institute provided a grant that greatly helped in the research of the project, while the editors of the journal *Research Studies* were kind enough to allow me to reproduce material that has appeared there. Finally, and most importantly, my wife Pat has been of such assistance that words cannot express my appreciation.

I

FOREIGN POLICY SPLITS
TWO DEMOCRATS

Harry S. Truman assumed the presidency on April 12, 1945, under tragic circumstances. Franklin Roosevelt, the nation's head of state since 1932, was dead, and the "man from Missouri" was the new leader. A grieved country held out its hand to this untried president and it seemed that he would need all the help that he could get. Speaking to a group of Senate pages and reporters on the day following his oath of office, Truman declared, "Boys . . . if you ever pray, pray for me now. I don't know whether you fellows ever had a load of hay fall on you, but when they told me yesterday what had happened, I felt like the moon, the stars, and all the planets had fallen on me. I've got the most terribly responsible job a man ever had." [1] And indeed there are few if any who would question the president's assessment of his new position. Truman inherited the challenges and problems involved in ending the war as well as the difficulties inherent in planning for the postwar world. Decisions had to be made and the new president did not flinch from making them as the months wore on. Truman quickly assured the country that he meant to carry on FDR's policies, and he set that program in motion. The use of the atomic bomb, the cessation of hostilities, and the plans for the creation of a United Nations seemed to fit the pattern that FDR would have followed. But after the fighting ended, Truman ran into problems that proved very unsettling to his administration.

By 1948 one of the key problems facing the Democrats was a threatened split in the classic New Deal coalition that took form with the emergence of a third party led by Henry A. Wallace. Wallace had served as secretary of agriculture in the Roosevelt administration before becoming vice-president during FDR's third term. However, in 1944 Wallace was dropped from the national ticket and was appointed secretary of commerce after Roosevelt's fourth victory. Wallace was in this position when Harry Truman took the reins of government in 1945.[2] By the end of 1947 the former vice-president was so critical of the Truman administration that he was willing to champion a movement that in many respects was an outcropping of the Democratic left.

On December 29, 1947, Henry Wallace informed the nation via coast-to-coast radio that he would seek the presidency on an independent ticket. The politically knowledgeable were not caught unaware, for Wallace's differences with the administration over foreign policy were well known. Essentially he was dissatisfied with Truman's handling of affairs with Russia. In his announcement Wallace made a forceful attempt to link the president to a war-oriented point of view.

> The luke warm liberals sitting on two chairs say, "why throw away your vote?" I say a vote for a new party in 1948 will be the most valuable vote you ever have cast or ever will cast. The bigger the peace vote in 1948, the more definitely the world will know that the United States is not behind the bi-partisan reactionary war policy which is dividing the world into two armed camps and making inevitable the day when American soldiers will be lying in their Arctic suits in the Russian snow. There is no real fight between a Truman and a Republican. Both stand for a policy which opens the door to war in our lifetime and makes war certain for our children.[3]

In domestic policy Wallace struck at racial discrimination, high prices, and the plight of the workingman,[4] but the real thrust of his challenge was concerned with the cold war. He elaborated on his stands in the January 5 edition of *New Republic,* which he was then editing. Peace and prosperity were the crucial issues at hand, and Wallace maintained that prosperity could not be attained until peace was a fact of life.[5]

The former vice-president's stand was actually quite predictable. Since 1946 he had been drifting away from the administration, and this drift culminated in his 1948 presidential bid. Therefore, an account of the events that transpired between the two men in 1946 is necessary for an understanding of the national politics of Wallace and Truman in 1948.

When Truman came to power Wallace was retained as secretary of commerce. During 1945 the secretary had generally remained quiet,[6] but that restraint changed the following year. In 1946 Wallace began issuing statements on foreign policy, especially regarding Soviet-American relations. Wallace, for example, believed that Winston Churchill was taking advantage of President Truman when the former prime minister delivered his much celebrated "Iron Curtain" speech in Fulton, Missouri, on March 5, 1946. In that speech Churchill argued that military action was needed to quell the expansionist tendencies of the Soviet Union; a tough approach was required to keep the Russians in their place. According to Barton Bernstein, "While he said that it was 'not our duty *at this time* . . . to interfere forcibly in the internal affairs' of Eastern Europe countries, Churchill implied that intervention was advisable when Anglo-American forces were strengthened."[7] Bernstein also points out that Truman was seated on the speaker's platform during the talk, a fact that many assumed to be a tacit endorsement by Truman of Churchill's views.[8] Writing to Mexican President Manuel Camacho on March 21, Wallace informed the Mexican leader that he personally deplored what Churchill had said. Further, he had the following to say with respect to Truman: "Confidentially, I may say that I told President Truman that Churchill by taking advantage of his hospitality had insulted him by making the speech in his presence at Fulton, Missouri. The President then informed me that

Churchill had not shown him the speech in advance; that all
he had done was to say that he was going to speak in behalf
of good relations between the United States and England." [9]
Wallace concluded by saying that he wanted to go to all
the countries of Latin America to counter the impressions
that Churchill had created. [10]

In July Wallace put his thoughts on paper and sent a long
letter to President Truman which derived from an earlier
letter sent to the president on March 14, 1946. [11] The July
document had much planning and thought behind it, as is
evidenced by a four-page memorandum written by Wallace
aide Richard Hippelheuser who analyzed it in great detail. [12]
The letter ran twelve pages; it called for the establishment of
friendlier relations with the Soviet Union, and the key to
those friendlier relations was to be a changed attitude on the
part of the United States. Wallace began by stating his reasons for writing:

> I have been increasingly disturbed about the trend of
> international affairs since the end of the war, and I am
> even more troubled by the apparently growing feeling
> among the American people that another war is coming
> and the only way we can head it off is to arm ourselves
> to the teeth. Yet all of past history indicates that an ar-
> maments race does not lead to peace but to war. The
> months just ahead may well be the crucial period which
> will decide whether the civilized world will go down in
> destruction after the five or ten years needed for several
> nations to arm themselves with atomic bombs. There-
> fore I want to give you my views on how the present
> trend toward conflict might be averted. [13]

He then presented specific proposals for getting along with
Russia based on control of atomic energy. Wallace believed
that an accord could be reached, but in order to do so, the
United States had to be flexible in its approach. "We must
be prepared to reach an agreement which will commit us to
disclosing information and destroying our bombs at a specific time or in terms of specific actions by other countries,

rather than at our unfettered discretion. If we are willing to negotiate on this basis, I believe the Russians will also negotiate seriously with a view to reaching an agreement." [14] The letter then argued that peace was the most important issue in the world at that time and the United States was in a position "to lead the world to peace." [15] Wallace's letter continued with a discussion of the policies the United States might pursue to strengthen relations with the USSR, including more economic interchange between the two countries. The last page of the correspondence contained a summary in which Wallace acknowledged that he was calling for something new: "This proposal admittedly calls for a shift in some of our thinking about international matters. It is imperative that we make this shift. We have little time to lose. Our postwar actions have not yet been adjusted to the lessons to be gained from experience of Allied cooperation during the war and the facts of the atomic age." [16]

Harry Truman responded to the July 23 proposals in a cordial but circumspect way. "Thank you for your long and thoughtful letter of July 23rd on the Russian question. I appreciate your taking the time to set out your views so thoroughly. I have been giving this entire subject a great deal of thought and I shall continue to do so." [17] Truman, however, was more candid and direct in his memoirs: he wrote in 1955 that Wallace had been willing to give in to the Russians in order to achieve a better world situation.[18] Truman's disagreements with the secretary's views were probably as pronounced in the summer of 1946 as they were when his memoirs appeared, but in those summer months while the president and the secretary held different foreign policy outlooks, events were such that they could live together in harmony for a while—though as it turned out, only a very short while.

On September 12, 1946, the tensions between Wallace and the administration came to the surface at New York City's Madison Square Garden. Speaking before a meeting sponsored by the Independent Citizens Committee of the Arts, Sciences and Professions, and the National Citizens Political

Action Committee (NCPAC), the secretary of commerce spoke about problems in American foreign policy. Wallace at first had wanted to speak about the record of the Seventy-eighth Congress, but Beanie Baldwin, a director of NCPAC, had persuaded him to base the speech on the July 23 letter.[19]

> Certainly we like the British people as individuals. But to make Britain the key to our foreign policy would be, in my opinion, the height of folly. We must not let the reactionary leadership of the Republican party force us into that position. We must not let British balance-of-power manipulations determine whether and when the United States gets into war.
>
> Make no mistake about it—the British imperialistic policy in the Near East alone, combined with Russian retaliation, would lead the United States straight to war unless we have a clearly-defined and realistic policy of our own. . . .
>
> We must not let our Russian policy be guided or influenced by those inside or outside the United States who want war with Russia. This does not mean appeasement.[20]

But the September 12 address contained more than a discussion of U.S.–British relations with respect to Russia. Wallace also attacked what he called the "get tough" policy with the Soviet Union. " 'Getting tough' never bought anything real and lasting—whether for schoolyard bullies or businessmen or world powers. The tougher we get, the tougher the Russians will get." [21] The secretary further maintained that the real peace in the world had to be between the United States and Russia, and in trying to reach such a state, it was of the utmost importance that America understand that nations with different economic systems could live in peace together.[22] He concluded by saying that peace would be the key issue of the 1946 Congressional elections as well as of the 1948 presidential election.[23]

Wallace also attacked the military. He argued that "Only the United Nations should have atomic bombs and its military establishment should give special emphasis to air power. It should have control of the strategically located air bases with which the United States and Britain have encircled the world." [24] He also stated that countries should not be allowed to build "atomic bombs, guided missiles and military aircraft for bombing purposes." [25]

To say the least, the speech greatly embarrassed the administration. Wallace always contended both privately and publicly that he and Truman had gone over the address in detail before it was presented.[26] On November 12, 1946, in private correspondence, he revealed his version of what had transpired at a meeting he had had with the president two days before the speech was given.

> In the final analysis the President of the United States is his own State Department. During the past year I have had up with Mr. Truman the question of relations with Russia many times. I had given him my letter of July 23 and he had read the opening paragraphs of it in my presence. Later on he acknowledged this letter. On September 10 we went over my speech together, paragraph by paragraph. He had one copy of it and I had the other. When we came to the paragraph which said, "I am neither pro-British nor anti-British. I am neither pro-Russian nor anti-Russian," he made the exclamation, "That is exactly my policy." I said, "Do you want me to say so?" He said, "Yes, I would like to have you put that in your speech." [27]

The president changed his position, according to Wallace, because of pressure put on him by men who favored a tough policy toward the Soviet Union.[28] In 1948, Wallace publicly argued as follows:

> What caused my resignation, however, were certain sentences in my September 12 speech, which had been cleared face to face with President Truman on September 10. These sentences disturbed Secretary Byrnes and Senator Vandenberg in Paris—not because of the fact that I said them, but because President Truman said at

a press conference that he had read my speech and approved it.

The key sentences were the following:

"The real peace treaty we now need is between the United States and Russia. On our part we should recognize that we have no more business in the *political* affairs of Eastern Europe than Russia has in the *political* affairs of Latin America, Western Europe, and the United States. We cannot permit the door to be closed to our trade, in Eastern Europe any more than we can in China. But at the same time we have to recognize that the Balkans are closer to Russia than to us—and that Russia cannot permit either England or the United States to dominate the politics of that area." [29]

And in a 1956 *Life* Magazine article the former vice-president reiterated the fact that he had gone over the speech with Truman two days before it was presented.[30] But there is another side to the story: Harry Truman's own explanation of what happened differs markedly from that of Wallace.

The president in his memoirs maintains that Wallace spent fifteen minutes with him on September 10 with the very last part of the meeting used for a discussion of the impending speech. "Just before he left, however, Wallace mentioned that he would deliver a speech in New York on the twelfth. He said that he intended to say that we ought to look at the world through American eyes rather than through the eyes of a pro-British or rabidly anti-Russian press. I told him that I was glad he was going to help the Democrats in New York by his appearance. There was, of course, no time for me to read the speech, even in part." [31] However, on the day the speech was to be delivered, Mr. Truman held a news conference at which he was asked about the forthcoming talk.

Q: In the middle of the speech are these words, "When President Truman read these words, he said they represent the policy of his administration."
The President: That is correct.

Q: My question is, does that apply just to that paragraph, or to the whole speech?
The President: I approved the whole speech.[32]

On the fourteenth the president found it necessary to clarify his remarks. Speaking to a group of newsmen at the White House, he informed them that he had been misunderstood at his press conference. He had merely approved of Wallace's right to give such an address. It did not reflect the foreign policy of the United States. There had been no change in the nation's foreign policy.[33]

There has been a natural misunderstanding regarding the answer I made to a question asked at the Press conference on Thursday, September twelfth, with reference to the speech of the Secretary of Commerce delivered in New York later that day. The question was answered extemporaneously and my answer did not convey the thought that I intended it to convey.

It was my intention to express the thought that I approved the right of the Secretary of Commerce to deliver the speech. I did not intend to indicate that I approved the speech as constituting a statement of the foreign policy of this country.

There has been no change in the established foreign policy of our government.[34]

Truman explained away his press conference remarks by writing in his memoirs essentially what he had said at the time, that is, that he should have been more explicit concerning the fact that he had simply been informed of the speech but had not seen a copy of it. Further, Mr. Truman said, "To make things worse, when Wallace delivered the speech, which was an all-out attack on our foreign policy, he said at the most critical point in the speech that he had talked to me in this vein and that I had approved of what he was saying." [35] The discrepancies between the Truman and Wallace accounts indicate that no clear understanding between the two had been reached before the speech was given. It is inconceivable that the president could have paid careful attention to a reading of the talk and then given it a hearty endorsement. At the same time, it is inconceivable to think that Wallace would have fabricated the entire episode, with Mr. Truman so readily available for comment. The results of this mix-up, however, were initially more serious for the administration, as Truman was left to untangle the web that had been spun.

The situation seemed to be going from bad to worse for the administration. On September 16 Wallace issued a public statement saying that he stood by his speech.[36] On the next day the July 23 letter was "leaked" to the press. White House aide George Elsey summed up the situation in a note, apparently written to record his own thoughts, entitled "l'Affaire Wallace." "Now it becomes apparent to the public and to the world that Truman has known Wallace's views for a long time, long before he saw the draft of the New York speech, and he is more than ever saddled with the Wallace point of view." [37] The administration was being pressured to take decisive action, for on September 18 Secretary of State James Byrnes wired the president from Paris threatening to resign if the secretary of commerce was not restrained while still a member of the Cabinet. Byrnes was supported in his position by Senators Arthur Vandenberg and Thomas Connally who were with him in Paris for a peace conference.[38] Byrnes argued that Wallace's speech had criticized U.S. policy as being too "harsh" toward Russia. He told the president that "At this critical time, whoever is Secretary of State must be known to have the undivided support of your administration and so far as possible, of the Congress." [39] September 18 was also notable because Wallace announced that he had agreed, after a White House conference with the president, to remain publicly silent until the conclusion of the Paris meeting of foreign ministers.[40] Two days later Truman requested and received Wallace's resignation. The president pointed out that there was a "fundamental conflict" between the administration's views on foreign policy and those of

Wallace.[41] He summed up his feelings to his mother and sister.

> Well I had to fire Henry today, and of course I hated to do it. Henry Wallace is the best Secretary of Agriculture this country ever had. . . .
>
> Henry is the most peculiar fellow I ever came in contact with. I spent two hours and a half with him Wednesday afternoon arguing with him to make no more speeches on foreign policy—or to agree to the policy for which I am responsible—but he wouldn't. So I asked him to make no more speeches until Byrnes came home. He agreed to that, and he and Charles Ross and I came to what we thought was a firm commitment that he'd say nothing beyond the one sentence statement we agreed he should make. Well, he answered questions and told his gang over at Commerce all that had taken place in our interview. It was all in the afternoon Washington News yesterday, and I never was so exasperated since Chicago. So—this morning I called Henry and told him he'd better get out, and he was so nice about it I almost backed out!
>
> Well, now he's out, and the crackpots are having conniption fits. I'm glad they are. It convinces me I'm right.[42]

Henry Wallace spoke of his experience on September 20, airing his views to millions of Americans via radio. He claimed that Truman's request for his resignation meant that he was free to speak out publicly on foreign policy matters— and that he did. "I feel our present foreign policy does not recognize the basic realities which led to two world wars and which now threatens another war—this time an atomic war." [43] Wallace as a private citizen could now present views with the aim of convincing the American people that his notions were more in keeping with the spirit of peace than were those of Harry Truman.

Shortly after his dismissal from the Cabinet, Wallace agreed to become editor of the *New Republic,* a post he would hold throughout 1947. The former vice-president, of course, had a marked national reputation, leading Michael Straight, the editor of the journal, to conclude that Wallace's name would bring an increased circulation to his magazine.[44] Upon hearing of Wallace's new role, Supreme Court Justice Franklin Murphy wrote what many must have felt. "This is just a note of cheer and good wishes. I believe the New Republic will offer you the forum for free expression which is the most important thing in our land, to those of high position as well as the humble. We must all feel that we are in no kind of spiritual or intellectual strait jacket."[45] Wallace answered by saying that "The glory of the American way of life is that we can still find ways of speaking frankly. I trust that as we exercise this God-given privilege, we shall do it on behalf of the general welfare."[46]

Even though his stand was a minority one and disfavored by most, Wallace could take heart in the fact that his arguments had struck a cord that appealed to many. On the day after the Madison Square Garden affair, the vice-chairman of the American Veterans Committee praised the speech for giving "new hope" to Americans who believed that peace between the United States and Russia was still attainable.[47] And on September 18 the noted scientist Albert Einstein wrote of the July 23 letter. "I cannot refrain from expressing to you my high and unconditional admiration for your letter to the President of July 23rd. There is a deep understanding concerning the factual and psychological situation and a far-reaching perception of the fateful consequences of present American foreign policy. Your courageous intervention deserves the gratitude of all of us who observe the present attitude of our government with grave concern."[48] As if such praise were not enough, on October 3, *Negro Digest* asked Wallace to write an article on "the Negro's stake in world peace" because in part "there is no doubt that the majority of Negroes consider you a great liberal."[49] Wallace had the opportunities to speak, but would he be heard?

In late September Wallace maintained to Max Lerner of *PM* that he was satisfied with the way things had worked out. "After recent events, I am, in retrospect, very happy. The cause of peace has been strengthened. The chance of war has been lessened." [50] Wallace's optimism was unjustified but he apparently believed that his views were important in keeping the United States from clashing head on with Russia. To British Parliament Member Donald Bruce, he observed that he had not realized how imperialistic the United States had become until he delivered his speech.[51] And to another correspondent he confided that "Truman is too much in the hands of the military." [52] Thus by late 1946, a definite break between Truman and Wallace had occurred, but at that point, Wallace had left only the administration; he was still a member of the Democratic party. Could he effect change from within the Democratic party and from his post at the *New Republic?* The answer became apparent by December 1947.

II

1947: AN EVENTFUL YEAR

Harry Truman's actions in 1947, that is, the enunciation of the Truman Doctrine, the veto of the Taft-Hartley bill, and the push for the economic recovery of Europe through massive aid under the Marshall Plan, helped to keep most Democrats in the party, but some were not won over by the president's actions. Henry A. Wallace was one man in this latter group. Throughout 1947 Wallace continued to assess his political fortunes, and finally toward the end of the year decided to challenge the Democrats by leading a third party. What follows is a description of administration and Wallace maneuvering during that eventful year.

Wallace's departure from the Cabinet in September 1946 seemed a blessing to many who pictured the former vice-president or some other prominent liberal as a replacement for Harry Truman on the Democratic ticket in 1948. Robert W. Kenny, attorney general of California from 1943 through 1946 and a Wallace supporter in 1948, revealed his feelings regarding the political situation as of October 1946. Kenny had just returned from a meeting of progressives held in Chicago when he wrote: "The general sense of the meeting was that there should be no attempt to start a third party and that the progressives would have a real chance to stage a revolt and capture the Democratic party in 1948. To them and me Truman now appears so weak that a strenuous drive to re-nominate him cannot be made and that the field will be open for the naming of a progressive candidate who will give the Democrats greater hope for victory." [1] Third party movements were dangerous, almost always ending in disaster for the new party, and professional politicians like Kenny knew it. However, reflecting on his remarks, it seems incredibly naive for Kenny to have believed that an incumbent president who controlled the party machinery could have been so easily removed in an election year. His enthusiasm for a candidate other than Truman overshadowed his sense of political reality in 1946.

During 1946 and most of 1947, Wallace, in his role as critic of American foreign policy, explicitly refrained from declaring that he would lead a third party in 1948. In fact, on October 6, 1946, he wrote to Cyril Clemens, president of the International Mark Twain Society that "There is nothing to the story that Senator Pepper and I are forming a third party." [2] At the beginning of 1947 the former vice-president's views had not fully changed, but he was dropping hints that a time might come when a new political organization would be needed in the country.

> I still think, as I told the PCA (Progressive Citizens of America) group here in New York on December 29, that the best bet is try to make the Democratic Party into a truly liberal party. I also said, however, that I did not believe in the one-party system and that a continuation of the present bi-partisan bloc might make it necessary for the liberals to find some other mechanism through which to make themselves felt in national affairs. I wonder if the Democrats realize how great is the danger to our party in the continuation of the present bi-partisan bloc tactics. In other words, I am just as much against a strong conservative Democratic Party as I am against a strong conservative Republican Party. If the Democratic Party is not going to become genuinely progressive, the quicker it dies the better. [3]

Commenting on this letter, the Schapsmeier brothers have concluded that Wallace was becoming less loyal to the Democratic party than he had previously been. [4] While the Schapsmeiers are correct in their assessment, the letter also shows that Wallace was still willing to fight from within the party as long as he perceived a chance of bringing about meaning-ful change. It is incorrect to think that Wallace had decided to launch a third party drive in early 1947. This decision came much later and only after the former vice-president was convinced that the Democrats had to be challenged by a lib-eral group galvanized into a new political party.[5]

Throughout 1947 Wallace proceeded with criticism of the administration. Using the *New Republic* as his platform, he continued to fire salvos at Truman's policies. He also trav-eled abroad and throughout the United States in a full at-tempt to get his message to the people, but he held back from *directly* linking himself to a third party. On June 5, speaking at the home of Josephus Daniels in Raleigh, North Carolina, Wallace responded to a question regarding a possible third party effort by saying "I'm doing everything I can to make the Democratic Party a liberal party. If the Democratic Party becomes a war party, a party of reaction and depression, then I'll no longer be a Democrat." [6] At the same time the former vice-president was also reported to have said that he would not support Harry Truman in 1948 and that he did not see himself working for a Republican in the election. At this point then, Wallace was narrowing his options. If the Demo-cratic party did not respond to his criticisms he would get out and go his own way.

Wallace's only chance of effecting change within the Demo-cratic party depended on his ideas being accepted by the party's leaders. However, this acceptance seemed highly un-likely since the president himself had removed Wallace from the Cabinet in 1946, making the following comments about him the day before he was asked to resign.

> I am not sure he is as fundamentally sound intellectu-ally as I had thought. He advised me that I should be as far to the "left" when Congress was not in session and that I should move right when Congress is on hand and in session. He said F.D.R. did that and that F.D. never let his "right" hand know what his "left" hand did. X is

a pacifist 100 percent. He wants us to disband our armed forces, give Russia our atomic secrets and trust a bunch of adventurers in the Kremlin Politbureau. I do not understand a "dreamer" like that. The German-American Bund under Fritz Kuhn was not half so dangerous. The Reds, phonies and the "parlor pinks" seem to be banded together and are becoming a national danger.

I am afraid they are a sabotage for Uncle Joe Stalin. They can see no wrong in Russia's four and one-half million armed force, in Russia's loot of Poland, Austria, Hungary, Rumania, Manchuria. They can see no wrong in Russia's living off the occupied countries to support the military occupation.[7]

These sentiments were obviously not those of a leader who would be about to embrace his critic's advice. But during 1947 Truman remained publicly silent or conciliatory toward his ex-secretary of commerce, a difficult task since Wallace was constantly attacking the administration's handling of foreign affairs.

The Truman administration's policies could do nothing but drive Wallace further from its camp. On March 12, the president appeared before a joint session of Congress requesting funds for financial, economic, and military aid to Greece and Turkey to prevent those nations from being overrun by Communists.[8] The Truman Doctrine, as this policy came to be called, was the first implementation of the containment concept—a far-reaching plan that would guide the United States through the cold war. Wallace was critical of the Truman Doctrine from the first, and he took to the air waves on March 13 saying, "I say this policy is utterly futile. . . . The world is hungry and insecure, and the people of all lands demand change. American loans for military purposes won't stop them. President Truman cannot prevent change in the world any more than he can prevent the tide from coming in or the sun from rising. But once America stands for opposition to change we are lost. America will become the most hated nation in the world." [9] Truman ignored this criticism and remained silent with respect to Wallace on this issue.

In April, Wallace went to Europe and continued the attacks on Truman.[10] Still Truman remained unruffled in public and even seemed friendly toward his adversary. On April 10, the president had the following exchange at his press conference while Wallace was off on his international junket.

> Q: Would you care to comment on the status of Senator Pepper and Wallace as members in good standing of the Democratic Party?
> The President: Mr. Pepper was at the Democratic dinner the other night, and I received him very cordially. I have no desire to read anybody out of the Democratic Party.
> Q: Does that go for Mr. Wallace too, Mr. President?
> The President: Certainly.
> Q: Would you like to have him campaign on the Democratic ticket next year, Mr. President?
> The President: We will take care of that situation when it arises. I think they will probably campaign for the Democratic ticket.[11]

Truman's remarks led *New York Times* columnist Felix Belair, Jr., to report that the president had extended an olive branch to Wallace and Pepper. "It was Mr. Truman's first conciliatory gesture toward the former Vice-President and Secretary of Commerce since dismissing him from the cabinet for misrepresenting American foreign policy last September. Although made casually at the regular White House news conference it was understood to have followed a careful weighing of Mr. Wallace's assets and liabilities as a campaign speaker." [12] The analysis seemed to make good sense at the time.

The White House wanted to be very careful in dealing with Wallace. Democratic leaders knew that many voters associated him with the New Deal, and they probably did not want to risk a final rupture with him for fear of losing many of these voters. The kind of grass-roots support Wallace had is illustrated by the following two letters. In the first, written two days after Wallace's criticism of the Truman Doctrine, the writer praised him for his "marvellous attack on Truman's blundering, sickening reversal of foreign policy." The letter then continued, "Unless you assume the active leadership of the fight against these little men, I fear that the American people will be led into a deep abyss of war, depression and thought control.

"No American wants war, the loss of his job or a giant fear hanging over his head. We are looking to you for leadership." [13] The second letter requested Wallace to speak at a fall 1947 American Labor party election rally to be held in Westchester County, New York: "We feel that your appearance could do more to unite and invigorate progressive forces in this area than any other event we could project. I think we can fairly claim that in this country we are the only political party which proudly acknowledges the purpose of attempting to achieve the social program of the late President Roosevelt, the program which now bears your name." [14] Aware that some voters thought in this way the administration had to act in a judicious manner with regard to public discussion of Wallace.

The president's desire to keep on decent terms with Wallace manifested itself once again during the week of April 14, 1947. On this occasion a *Baltimore Sun* correspondent pointed out that Truman had attempted to bypass conflict with Wallace, who at the time was still blasting U.S. policy in Europe, by cancelling his weekly news conference, and refraining from engaging in a question and answer session at his yearly meeting with the American Society of Newspaper Editors. [15] Openly the president seemed intent on avoiding the catastrophic confrontation that seemed inevitable. Perhaps, the White House felt that given enough rope, Wallace might do himself in. In other words, because of his sharply critical attacks on government policy he might alienate Americans rather than win their support, for history had shown that the

American people stood by their government in times of peril. This the Democrats believed was just such a time.[16]

Yet, while the president's public actions indicated an unhostile attitude toward Wallace, his private actions revealed a rather different picture. Under criticism in some circles for his handling of domestic affairs, the president nonetheless had a great deal of support for his foreign policy stands, the Wallace group not withstanding. On March 28, 1947, Secretary of the Navy James Forrestal gave Presidential Press Secretary Charles Ross some excerpts of a letter that had been written to *New York Times* writer Arthur Krock. The author of the letter, obviously pleased with Truman's work, wrote, "I am a Democrat although I opposed President Roosevelt in his last three elections. I am strong for Harry Truman. He is making the kind of President I wanted FDR to be. I want to help him. He is growing in strength in the West. His chances are getting better all the time for 1948." [17] These words are not of earth shattering consequence and should not be taken as such, but they do demonstrate that the tough stand taken by the administration toward Russia had the potential of paying high political dividends. Truman could peruse sentiments like this and more easily let Wallace go his own way.

On April 9 Truman received a wire from Alabama Congressman Frank Boykin concerning remarks that Wallace had been making. Boykin, long critical of the former vice-president, explained, "In my opinion, he is not and has never been a true Democrat and has done more to hurt the Democratic Party than anyone I know." [18] The representative from Alabama had also noted that Wallace was going to Europe (although Wallace had actually already arrived in London on April 8) and suggested that the president or the state department issue statements declaring that Wallace did not speak for the government.[19] The president answered by avoiding mention of Boykin's comment or suggestion. Politely, Truman said, "I appreciate very much your telegram. . . . It was kind and thoughtful for you to go to so much trouble." [20] However, later in the month the president received a letter that he did answer in a more affirmative fashion. It praised him for not attacking Wallace: "This is just a note of commendation for your refusal to spank Henry Wallace.

"In the language of your old friend, Senator Stone, he apparently is suffering physical disability in the form of 'a diarrhea of words and a constipation of ideas.' "[21] And Truman's reply was short and to the point. "I certainly appreciated your note of April nineteenth, in regard to Henry. The Senator's comments seem to fit him exactly."[22] The president's words indicate that privately, at least, he anything but accepted Wallace's criticisms.

Truman's antagonism toward Wallace became a matter of public record in late May. On April 14, 1947, Louis E. Starr commander of the Veterans of Foreign Wars, wrote to Truman complaining about Wallace's European speeches. Starr concluded his piece by stating, "It is my suggestion that in order to relieve the governments, of Great Britain and France, as well as their people, of the embarrassment of Mr. Wallace's presence and inflammatory statements that his passport be revoked by the United States and that he should have no further standing as a visitor with the official sanction and approval of the United States Government."[23] Two days later Truman replied to Starr's letter. After a first paragraph that discussed freedom of expression, the president got down to the remarks that were to be later spotlighted. "There is not very much that can be done about Henry's wild statements and if I take notice of them it only gives him more publicity. He does not represent anybody in the Government of the United States and, therefore, we can take no notice of it."[24] On May 28 columnist Robert S. Allen reported that Truman had written a letter to the VFW commander which denounced Wallace. Allen commented that "It is the first time Mr. Truman has put himself on record assailing Mr. Wallace's widely publicized campaign against the administration's foreign policy, and signifies an open break with them."[25] Allen's judgment with respect to the letter was misleading.

The president had indeed criticized Wallace, but he had also defended his right to speak freely. The evidence, however, does show that while Truman was merely expressing his personal opinion about Wallace, he was critical of his ideas on foreign policy. This criticism meant that the Democrats would have to figure out a plan to deal with Wallace while he was still a member of their party.

By June, there could be little doubt that Wallace was more than a nuisance. Even though he had made no definite move toward a third party, Democrats were showing political wisdom by keeping a watchful eye on him. On June 6, George Elsey, aide to presidential advisor Clark Clifford, sent Clifford two documents concerned with Wallace's actions and their implications with respect to administration policy.[26] One of these was a memo dated June 2, 1947, written by a Gael Sullivan, executive director of the Democratic National Committee.[27] Sullivan began by saying that "Wallace is not a minor consideration in the 1948 campaign!" and that while his European tour had been less than successful, his tour of the United States, then in progress, "has been effective." [28] Sullivan used newspaper reports as evidence to show that Wallace was gaining support from within the Democratic party. He then wrote,

> There is no question that Wallace has captured the imagination of a strong segment of the American public. His meetings have been well attended. Much of the enthusiasm has been stage managed by Communists. The chanting and the cheering have all the appearance of staged events. But this does not explain the crowds.
>
> These crowds are made up of rabid left wingers. But there is a substantial group of isolationists and conservatives there too. This group feels strongly that the Truman policy means war.
>
> They were present honestly to protest against such a policy.
>
> There are many veterans who feel the same way.
>
> Let's face it. The veterans of World War II don't

relish any thought of another war. They know how tough the Russians are.[29]

Sullivan then continued to cite growing momentum for Wallace across the country and concluded with the following comments:

> Wallace is a major consideration in 1948!
>   Something should be done to combat him.
>   The President should:
> 1) Go on the air in a series of fireside chats which would explain and implement the Truman policy.
> 2) The non-military side of the Truman Doctrine should be accented.
> 3) Wallace's fuzzy thinking should be answered by clear level-headed replies—ignoring the man but answering the issue.
> 4) Adequate thought should be given to decide whether Wallace is wanted BACK AND SOMETHING SHOULD BE done about it before he gets himself too far committed to a Third party. . . .
>   Action should be taken either to
> 1) Appease Wallace
>   or
> 2) Pull the rug on him.[30]

The memo indicates that decisions being made at the national level were in some ways influenced by the spectre of growing Wallace support in 1947.

The impact of Wallace was most certainly present with respect to Truman's veto of the Taft-Hartley bill on June 20. Traditionally, since the days of the New Deal, the Democratic coalition had been in part made up of organized labor, but during the early period of the Truman administration it appeared that this group might desert. The president himself had caused much alienation when, in May 1946, he threatened to draft railway strikers to end a railroad strike.[31] At that time A. F. Whitney, president of the Brotherhood of Railway Trainmen, promised to spend his union's entire treasury of $47,000,000 to defeat Truman in 1948.[32] In retrospect this appears to have been the low point of relations between organized labor and the administration.

In 1947, however, the president was ready to make a strong attempt to regain labor support. The Taft-Hartley veto, a major victory for his liberal advisers, was the key to this action as well as an important step in cutting possible labor support for Henry Wallace. *Time* Magazine in commenting on the veto explained, "Harry Truman's political motives were fairly sound: 1) he would win back labor's support missing in 1946; 2) he would cut the underpinning out from Henry Wallace and collapse the third party which some dissident New Dealers were jerry-building." [33] Professor R. Alton Lee, who has produced a volume dealing specifically with the administration and Taft-Hartley, has shown that there were many political factors that the president considered before his veto.[34] One of these focused on the boost that Truman's approval of the bill would have given to Wallace. According to Lee, Robert Hannegan, then Democratic national chairman, had telephoned Truman and had told him that by signing the Taft-Hartley bill into law he would hand Wallace "the domestic issue that he needed to start a third party." [35] There were also other good reasons for vetoing the measure. Disapproval would help guard against labor apathy in 1948 since the unions would have a great deal at stake. It would also show that the president was a friend of the worker. Finally, Truman's most important advisor, Clark Clifford, favored such a move.[36]

The veto of the bill was one of Truman's first campaign acts. It provided him with a key issue that later would be consistently used against the Republicans, but its more immediate effect was to strike at potential Wallace backing. Wallace himself conceded, "President Truman's veto of the Taft-Hartley labor bill has prolonged the life of the Democratic party. Signing the bill would have brought immediate action by organized labor for the formation of a third party." The former vice-president urged that the Democratic senators who voted to override the president's veto (eighteen of twenty from the South) be purged from the party.[37] There can be little doubt that Truman's action seriously injured Wallace's chances of heading a movement that would achieve a substantial following. The actual veto message was a scorching one in which the president made clear his objections to the bill and stated that it "would go far toward weakening our trade union movement." [38] Irwin Ross in his account of the 1948 election concluded that after the Taft-Hartley veto, most labor people gave up the idea of a third party, and without that support a third party had no chance of success.[39] Curtis MacDougall, the major chronicler of "Gideon's Army" asserts with certainty that "If he had not vetoed the Taft-Hartley Labor Act on June 20, 1947, Harry S. Truman would never have been elected President of the United States on November 2, 1948." [40] MacDougall then demonstrates that most labor union leaders fell in line behind the Democratic party. In fact, A. F. Whitney announced that the veto had vindicated Truman and that a third party was "out of the question." [41] MacDougall who was a member of the Progressive party explains that Wallace headed the new party fully aware of that fact that he did not have the support of any major labor leader in the country.[42]

Overall, Truman had done a good job of keeping New Dealers in his party. In early June the administration had stated its plan for the economic rebuilding of Western Europe (as enunciated by Secretary of State George C. Marshall on June 6, 1947), and most Americans endorsed it. However, by December 29 Wallace would say to the nation:

> But I have fought and shall continue to fight programs which give guns to people when they want plows. I fight the Truman Doctrine and the Marshall Plan as applied because they divide Europe into two warring camps. Those whom we buy politically with our food will soon desert us. They will pay us in the basic coin of temporary gratitude and then turn to hate us because our policies are destroying their freedom. We are restoring western Europe and Germany through United States'

agencies rather than United Nations' agencies because
we want to hem Russia in. We are acting in the same
way as France and England after the last war and the
end result will be the same—confusion, digression and
war.[43]

The majority of disgruntled Democrats wanted to work
within the confines of the party and would not join Wallace.
As James Roosevelt, the son of FDR and chairman of the
California Democratic State Central Committee, wrote to J.
Howard McGrath, the man who replaced Robert Hannegan
as chairman of the Democratic National Committee,

> A majority of us, with the organization of the present
> Democratic State Central Committee, made a successful
> beginning to eliminate the influences of this small mi-
> nority of conservative element and have devoted the in-
> tervening months in bringing our Party as close as pos-
> sible to the real interest of the people. We are deter-
> mined to continue that effort.
>
> We are determined to do it within the frame-work of
> the Democratic Party. That is why we have dis-associ-
> ated ourselves from Mr. Henry Wallace and his princi-
> pal backers in California, a small group now led by
> Robert W. Kenny.[44]

Truman had begun to polish his liberal image and the
voters were ready to accept the president's actions in that direction, but Henry A. Wallace was not. Wallace had continued to move cautiously with regard to a third party, but by
November, the former vice-president indicated that he would
lead such a venture.[45] Beanie Baldwin feels that Wallace ran
because he had so committed himself to the peace issue that
he felt he had to do something about it. Wallace wanted to
use the new party to force a shift in the direction that the
Truman administration had been heading and at the same
time lay the groundwork for an effective, future third party.[46]

On December 2, a private meeting was held in New York
City where Wallace announced to some of his intimates that
he would head a new political movement.[47] At that meeting,

Baldwin, who would serve as campaign manager for the new organization, presented a carefully worked out memo explaining just how the public should be made aware of Wallace's decision and when this task should be done.[48] With regard to the Democrats, Baldwin urged that Wallace's announcement "should precede Truman's message on the state of the union which will be delivered to Congress on January 5. It is important that our forces take initiative and not be placed in the position of answering what is likely to be a very demagogic speech by Truman, particularly as it will relate to domestic issues." [49] Wallace, with the support of the Progressive Citizens of America, felt that he could bring about a change in America.

Most observers believed that the formation of a new political party deriving from the left-leaning segments of the Democratic party was certain to be a severe blow to Democratic chances in 1948. Speculation had it that a new party would mean definite victory for the Republicans in 1948. Democratic Congresswoman Helen Gahagan Douglas of California expressed these sentiments to Wallace in a December 10 letter. "Just noticed the other day that you would shortly make the decision as to whether or not you would give your name to the leadership of the third party. I hope that you won't do so. As you remember, last spring I told you that I felt that a third party could do nothing but elect the worst possible Republican candidates an defeat the few liberal Congressmen we now have in Washington." [50] But this plea was too late as Wallace had already decided to try to liberalize American politics by reshaping foreign policy.

III

DEMOCRATIC STRATEGY: THE CLIFFORD MEMORANDUM ANALYZED

By 1947, Democratic party leaders were giving much thought to their party's possibilities in the upcoming national election —aside from the problems with Henry Wallace. The outcome of the 1946 Congressional elections had proven to some members of the administration that a new course of presidential political action was necessary if the Democrats were to triumph in 1948. Beginning in early 1947, informal meetings were held on Monday nights at the apartment of Oscar Ewing, director of the Federal Security Agency.[1] Meeting with Ewing were Clark Clifford, Leon Keyserling, C. Girard Davidson, David Morse, and Charles Murphy.[2] Clifford, who has characterized himself as the head of the liberal group in the administration in 1947,[3] argues that he and his associates wanted "to plot a coherent political course for the administration" with emphasis on domestic policy.[4] An infight between the forces led by Clifford and the more conservative thinkers headed by Secretary of the Treasury John Snyder had been raging, with the Clifford group wanting the president to strike out in a more liberal direction.[5] In the final analysis it was the liberal strategy that won, most probably due to the influence that Clark Clifford had as special counsel to the president.

Clifford's importance in the Truman victory of 1948 cannot be exaggerated. He was the number one campaign strategist, and because of his position as special counsel, he always had access to the president. His background showed little indication of the success he would enjoy on the national political scene. A graduate of the law school at Washington University in St. Louis, he had gone on to become a successful lawyer with a strong commitment to the New Deal. Before the Second World War, his political experience had been limited to one Congressional campaign. But in 1945, while serving in the Navy, Clifford was asked by James K. Vardaman, naval aide to Mr. Truman, to work at the White House as assistant naval aide. At thirty-nine years of age he was working in the highest echelon in government, but there was little for him to do at first because the president and many of his staff were at the Potsdam Conference. Consequently, Clifford began to help Truman's special counsel Samuel Rosenman. In June 1946 Clifford succeeded Rosenman in that post,[6] and the next year such popular magazines as *Life* and the *Saturday Evening Post* published feature stories on him, with *Life's* writer correctly calling Clifford "top advisor to the Truman administration." [7]

Clifford's thinking as well as that of other influential Democrats showed itself in a forty-three page confidential memorandum authored by the special counsel and presented to the president on or about November 19, 1947. This memo was actually a blueprint for Democratic strategy in 1948; and journalist Cabell Phillips, the first author to draw on the information contained in it, concludes that it had substantial influence and was "perhaps decisive" in Truman's campaign.[8] Clifford's gift was one of synthesis, for the ideas put forth in the memo could have come from any number of Democrats, says former Clifford aide, George M. Elsey.[9] The important fact is that Clifford gathered the thoughts and presented them in a coherent fashion to the president who was very much taken with the document.[10]

Clifford began by explaining that the memo could be entitled "The Politics of 1948" with its aim being to develop "a course of political conduct for the Administration extending from November, 1947 to November, 1948." [11] At the outset he stated that the "comments" rested on his assessment of the best political path to tread. Legitimizing his thought, he argued that "It may generally be assumed that the policy that is politically wise is also the best policy for this country." [12] This last bit of wisdom is, of course, highly questionable, but as the memo unfolds, it becomes clear that Clifford was interested in only one thing: achieving victory for Harry S. Truman!

The memorandum was divided into two parts: "The Probabilities" and "The Course of Action." It was conceived to give the most down to earth appraisal of the political situation as it then existed. Clifford's underlying thought was "that the Democratic Party is an unhappy alliance of Southern conservatives, Western progressives and Big City labor" with Party leaders holding these groups together for a victory in 1948. [13] In other words, the Democrats had to make certain that their coalition would continue to function in the election year.

Prediction number one according to Clifford was that Thomas E. Dewey would be the Republican presidential candidate. [14] From this correct diagnosis of what was to come from the GOP, Clifford moved to a discussion of the South, where his analysis eventually proved to be incorrect. *"President Truman will be elected if the Administration will successfully concentrate on the traditional Democratic alliance between the South and West.* It is inconceivable that any policies initiated by the Truman Administration no matter how 'liberal' could so alienate the South in the next year that it would revolt. As always, the South can be considered safely Democratic." [15] Looking back at this error in judgment many years later, Clifford could chuckle and simply say that he had been mistaken. [16] And as it turned out, Truman did not need the "solid South" to win.

Clifford then shifted his attention to the possibility of a Wallace candidacy, forecasting that the former vice-president would lead a third party in 1948. Because his appraisal was written in November 1947 Clifford was sticking his neck out by making such a prediction, and he seemed to know it. Acknowledging that "the majority of informed opinion" was in disagreement with his belief, he still felt that there were more factors pointing Wallace in a third party direction than there were militating against it.[17] Clifford began enumerating reasons why Wallace would run, beginning with a statement that the men close to Wallace were inspired by Communist party rhetoric, and these men wanted, according to the special counsel, to see the demise of the American economy.

> It [Moscow] is also convinced there is no longer any hope that the Truman Administration will submit to the Russian program of world conquest and expansion. From the Communist long-range point of view, there is nothing to lose and much to gain if a Republican becomes the next President. The best way it can help achieve that result, and hasten the disintegration of the American economy, is to split the Independent and labor union vote between President Truman and Wallace —and thus insure the Republican candidate's election.[18]

For Clifford this view of the Soviet Union was not new. In September 1946 at the request of the president he had done an analysis of Russian-American relations which helped shape the containment policy that the United States adopted to deal with perceived Russian aggression.[19] Clifford held to the immediate postwar view of Russia which maintained that the Soviets were bent on destroying the free world. Even in 1972 he argued that the Truman administration "saved the free world" from the Soviet Union.[20] This "hard-line" outlook was incorporated into his strategy for dealing with Wallace. Certainly with this kind of thinking going on in the highest circles of the Democratic party, it is apparent that Wallace had no chance of moving the Democrats on issues.

Clifford based his prediction about Wallace on his conclusion that the men around the ex–vice-president would convince him to run. He argued that friends of Wallace like C. B. Baldwin, Harold Young, and Michael Straight had so much influence on Wallace that they could persuade him that it was his duty to run.[21] He further suggested that Wallace's own thinking was propelling him toward a third party. "The most recent report on Wallace's personality by men who know him well are that while his mysticism increases, the humility which was once his dominant characteristic has decreased to the vanishing point; there is something almost Messianic in his belief today that he is the Indispensable Man." [22] Whether or not this statement about Wallace was true, Clifford built his prediction upon it.

Evidence was then presented against the possibility of a third party, but it was weak. Clifford countered his own negative thoughts by pointing to Wallace's Labor Day speech in Detroit where he made a threat about leading a dissident party.[23] He warned that it was "dangerously unrealistic" to discount talk of a third party simply because it was improbable that such a movement could get enough signatures to get on most ballots. Clifford made his point very forcefully. "Wallace is gambling for high stakes. He hopes to defeat President Truman by splitting the Democratic Party and then inherit its leadership so he can be the candidate of 1952." [24] Obviously the concern over Wallace was not that he could or would win the presidency in 1948, but rather that his candidacy would give the election to the Republicans. Clifford feared that Wallace might be able to draw enough votes away from Truman to cause the incumbent's defeat. It is also interesting to note that Clifford thought Wallace would be back in the Democratic party in 1952, and this event was something that he did not want to see occur.

The last two paragraphs of the prediction concerning Wallace were addressed to the Communist issue. Astutely, Clifford warned that it was unwise to picture all of Wallace's followers as Communists. While Communists were conspicuously present, Wallace also had numbers of genuine supporters, especially among the younger electorate. He advised that "In a close election, no votes can be ignored. The only safe working hypothesis is to assume *now* that Wallace will run on a third party ticket. Every effort must be made *now* jointly and at one and the same time—to dissuade him and also to identify him in the public mind with the Communists." [25] The strategy of identifying him with Communists is worth some discussion. What Clifford suggested was indeed good political thinking, but it certainly was something less than clean politics. A campaign planner has to make certain judgments concerning the tactics to be used for possible victory. For an individual with Clifford's outlook there was nothing wrong with the Democratic party engaging in baiting Wallace on the Communist issue. The Communists were the enemy and anti-Communism could pay substantial political dividends. Ironically the use of the anti-Communist issue would eventually come back to haunt the Truman administration during the McCarthy period in the early 1950s.

From the possibility of a Wallace candidacy Clifford moved to a discussion of independents, for it was the "independent and progressive voter" that would decide the election in 1948.[26] The analysis indicated that the president had to overtly seek out these voters, for "party organization" could no longer deliver the votes needed for victories. The emphasis was to be on "pressure groups," and those singled out for discussion were the farmer, labor, "liberals," Negro, Jewish, Catholic, Italian, and alien.[27]

Clifford's view of the farm group was at that moment optimistic but tempered with caution:

> The farmer is at least at present favorably inclined toward the Truman Administration. His crops are good. However the high prices may be affecting the rest of the people, they help him more than hurt him. Parity will protect him—and the Marshall Plan will aid him. The economic and political trend of the Administration (except its tax program) is going his way. Whether prosperity makes him the conservative he usually becomes in good times remains to be seen—but, if it does, nothing much can be done about it in terms of more political or economic favors to woo him back to the Democratic banner.[28]

Turning to labor, the memorandum argued that "President Truman and the Democratic Party cannot win without the *active* support of organized labor. It is dangerous to assume that labor now has nowhere else to go in 1948. *Labor can stay home.*" [29] Clifford was convinced that the Taft-Hartley veto had made labor sympathetic to the administration, but the real task was to keep this group behind the president in the election year. Interestingly enough, no mention was made of a possible labor defection to Wallace. Rather, an increased effort by Governor Dewey's supporters to garner labor backing was pointed out as a possibility. [30]

The liberals were discussed next. Clifford had great respect for this bloc and not for utopian reasons. They could be quite important in aiding the administration if they could be reached.

> The liberals are numerically small. But, similar to manufacturers and financiers of the Republican Party, they are far more influential than mere members entitle them to be. The businessman has influence because he contributes his money. The liberal exerts unusual influences because he is articulate. The "right" may have the money, but the "left" has always had the pen. If the "intellectual" can be induced to back the President, he will do so in the press, on the radio, and in the movies. He is the artist of propaganda. He is the "idea man" for the people. [31]

While not exactly enamored of the administration, most of these people could not support Wallace because of his foreign policy pronouncements and would not support the Republicans because of the actions of the Eightieth Congress. [32] Clifford obviously felt that it was the job of the Democratic party to actively solicit this group's help.

Clifford then turned to the minorities. Regarding the Negro, he argued, one could accept as true the theory that the Negro vote would act as a "balance of power" in New York, Illinois, Pennsylvania, Ohio, and Michigan. [33] The danger, as Clifford saw it, was not that the black vote would go to Wallace, but rather that the Negro would return to the Republican party. He indicated that conservative Southern Democrats had demonstrated that the Negro could expect very little from the party as a whole in the way of future gains. The Democrats could point to the advances since 1932, especially in the economic sphere, but so doing would not be enough. Clifford then issued a warning to the president:

> Unless the Administration makes a determined campaign to help the Negro (and everybody else) on the problems of high prices and housing—and capitalizes politically on its efforts—the Negro vote is already lost. Unless there are new and real efforts (as distinguished from mere political gestures which are today thoroughly understood and strongly resented by sophisticated Negro leaders), the Negro bloc, which, certainly in Illinois and probably in New York and Ohio, *does* hold the balance of power, will go Republican.[34]

This statement written in 1947 seems to negate the Wallace-Baldwin statement of November 4, 1948, which took credit for making Truman campaign for the "full civil rights of the Negro people." [35] A number of spectacular events would take place in 1948 with respect to civil rights, including the issuance of the executive order calling for desegregation of the armed forces and the executive order creating a Fair Employment Practices Committee within the government. However, it was not the Wallace candidacy that was the prime mover in these actions but rather the Republicans.

The Jewish vote was the next order of business in the memo: ". . . Insofar as it can be thought of as a bloc, (it) is important only in New York," wrote Clifford.[36] At that moment the most important issue for this group was Palestine, and he urged that the administration not yield to "political expediency" in making decisions concerning that country. His opinion was that the administration would derive more benefit from looking at the "intrinsic merit" of the situation.[37] By May 1948, though, Clifford had changed his view. As

Patrick Anderson writes: "In May, 1948, Clifford and (Oscar) Chapman persuaded Truman to override State Department objections and grant immediate recognition to the new state of Israel. They hoped a dramatic gesture of support to Israel would be repaid by Jewish votes and campaign contributions that fall." [38] Anderson, who interviewed Clifford, is convincing in his assessment of the role politics played in the recognition of Israel.

From the Jewish voter, Clifford turned to the traditional Democratic Catholic constituency. He maintained that the administration's stance toward Communism would be the decisive political issue for this group. And he believed that it would have a "definite appeal" to the country's Catholic population.[39] The Italians, another minority, had been Democratic since 1943, but at the time of Clifford's writing, some were displeased because of a "harsh" Italian peace treaty.[40] He offered no advice about dealing with this bloc.

The special counsel concluded his analysis of interest groups with a discussion of aliens. Those in favor of "expanded immigration quotas" were pro-administration, but they were also said to hold "a flexible position." [41]

The discussion of the various pressure groups operating in the American political arena indicated Clifford's grasp of political reality. He had presented the president with a clear picture of what things were like with respect to different segments of the American people as of November 1947.

The all important topic of foreign policy was the next order of business for Clifford. *"The foreign policy issues of the 1948 campaign will be our relations with the USSR and the Administration's handling of foreign reconstruction and relief,"* explained the memorandum.[42] Clifford was cynical about the continuation of bipartisanship in foreign policy, because of the upcoming presidential election. He therefore made some comments based on how Truman might benefit from the nation's encounters with Russia. On U.S. relations with the Soviets, Clifford's appraisal was candid and harsh to a degree that many today would find quite disturbing. He set forth the pragmatic liberal's anti-Communist arguments of the 1940s. From the following it is evident that Wallace never really had a chance of changing the president's foreign policy. "There is considerable political advantage to the Administration in its battle with the Kremlin. The best guess today is that our poor relations with Russia will intensify. The nation is already united behind the President on this issue. The worse matters get, up to a fairly certain point—real danger of imminent war—the more is there a sense of crisis. In times of crisis the American citizen tends to back up his President." [43] Without arguing that the United States should begin a war, this statement explains that it is politically expedient to keep cold war tensions with Russia at a near boiling point. In this manner the president could be assured of popular support and possible victory in 1948. Clifford's words indicate that there was a tie between foreign policy direction in terms of the cold war, and domestic political considerations. The memo also maintained that Truman's appointment of General George C. Marshall as secretary of state had been masterful in that it protected the president from criticism of his stand toward Russia. [44]

Focus then shifted from foreign policy to the domestic issues that would be of importance in 1948. Clifford alleged that "high prices and housing" were going to be the chief items but said that "The High Cost of Living will be the most controversial issue . . . indeed the *only* domestic issue." [45] The memorandum urged that the Democrats underscore the problem and make sure that their record was "crystal clear" to the voters. This record was to include a presidential proposal to Congress on price controls, which would serve as a "bold" step in dealing with the problem. [46]

The first section of Clifford's memo ended with a discussion of executive-congressional relations. Because of the election, Congress would not carry on much meaningful business. The president and the Congress would continue their battle because, in Clifford's estimation, both would be trying to establish campaign records upon which to run. The final statement in this section is worth citing in full because it demonstrates Clifford's general thinking for 1948.

> Insofar as it has control of the situation, the Administration should select the issues upon which there will be conflict with the majority of the Congress. It can assume it will get no major part of its own program approved. Its tactics must, therefore, be entirely different than if there were any real point to bargaining and compromise. Its recommendations—in the State of the Union Message and elsewhere—must be tailored for the voter, not the Congressman; they must display a label which reads "no compromises." The strategy on the Taft-Hartley Bill—refusal to bargain with the Republicans and to accept any compromises—paid big political dividends. The strategy should be expanded in the next session to include all the *domestic* issues.[47]

The president's special counsel had shaped a political strategy in which rhetoric was going to play the key role. The art of politics was practiced not to achieve compromise, but to achieve victory. Indeed, as a strategist Clifford showed a knack for knowing how to capture votes.

His predictions completed, Clifford began his discussion of "The Course of Action." This area was divided into "the political level" and "the program level." [48] Beginning with the political level, his first observation concerned the organization of the Democratic party. He viewed the party's leadership as "moribund" because the Democrats had been in power so long.[49] He recommended that a new chairman of the Democratic National Committee be appointed with all possible speed "to rebuild" and unify,[50] for without a degree of harmony and cohesiveness among its operatives, the Democratic party would have little chance of winning in 1948.

Clifford next dealt with *"Liaisons with Labor and Independents,"* and urged that the president invite labor leaders to the White House. "One by one they should be asked to 'come by' and the President should ask for their advice on matters *in general.* . . . No human being—as every President from Washington on has ruefully learned—can resist the glamour, the self-important feeling of 'advising' a President on anything." [51] Obviously those who thought that they were in advising positions would be sure to give support during the campaign. Clifford also advised that a "lieutenant" be appointed by Truman to work with labor. This person was to have "a fresh 'face' " and be trusted both by the president and labor leaders.[52] "A program of cultivation" was also suggested to be established for "the progressive and independent leaders around the country." Again, it was proposed that a lieutenant be appointed for each group who could act as a liaison. Clifford believed that this kind of system could keep the White House informed as to what these groups were thinking and saying. "These regular reports added to those made by a revitalized party organization will increase the Administration's political intelligence, today sadly atrophied." [53]

The memo continued with a discussion of former vice-president Wallace in a section called *"The Insulation of Henry Wallace."* Clifford's view was as follows:

> Wallace should be put under attack whenever the moment is psychologically correct. If it is clear that organizational work is being undertaken by his men in the West, either for a third party or for delegates to the Democratic Convention—and that work seems to be taking effect—the Administration must persuade prominent liberals and progressives—*and no one else*—to move publicly into the fray. They must point out that the core of the Wallace backing is made up of Communists and the fellow-travelers. At the same time, some lines should be kept out so that if the unpredictable Henry finally sees the light and can be talked into supporting the Administration, he will have a handy rope to climb back on the bandwagon—if he is wanted.[54]

Part of this strategy required that the president remain silent. It was up to "prominent liberals" to put Wallace on the firing line and only if he was perceived as a real threat. When asked

about this plan years later, Clifford explained that he had
had the press in mind for the liberal attack on Wallace.[55]
But no matter whom he had specifically in mind, a planned
liberal attack by the Democrats did not become necessary;
the recently formed Americans for Democratic Action (ADA)
took it upon themselves to make certain that the Wallaceites
did not injure the image of American liberalism. Throughout 1948 this organization waged a relentless fight against the
Progressive party. Clifford suggested the use of the Communist issue against Wallace, and indeed, the ADA employed
precisely this issue during the campaign.[56]

Clifford's political cunning with respect to Wallace is very
apparent in his proposal that a place be left open for Wallace
if he desired to come back home. All angles were covered by
the memo. If Wallace persisted in his ways and refused to cooperate, verbally attacking him would not be enough. In order to stop him, the president would have to move "left in
his appointments," which would undermine his attacks.[57]
Clifford pointed out that Wallace had raised the issue of "the
fear of Wall Street," an issue that was crucial to the Democratic party.[58] The president was vulnerable on this issue because many Democrats associated only Republicans with Wall
Street, but many prominent administration people had con-
nections there. Further, Wallace had linked Truman to
former President Herbert Hoover by reminding voters that
Hoover had frequented the White House.[59] In political dol-
lars and cents, Truman could not win without carrying the
West and to get the West he had to have a "liberal image."
The "Wall Street label" could be devastating in this situation.[60] Clifford maintained that while such charges might
be "unfair" to those under attack, politically they could be
disastrous for the administration. The strategy was not to
ignore the charges but to counter them by making progressive
appointments. "Top ranking appointments of men like
young Bob LaFollette are needed. The pattern must be re-
peated even if some of them are not confirmed. Under their
impact, Wallace will fade away." [61]

The creation of a presidential image—an image that would draw votes—was next considered.[62] The president was urged to put himself before the people in whatever way possible. "So a President who is also a candidate must resort to subterfuge—for he cannot sit silent. He must be in the limelight," and Truman had to "resort to the kind of trip which Roosevelt made famous in the 1940 campaign—the 'inspection tour.' " [63] The overall image to be worked for was one of presenting Truman as "a well-rounded broad-gauged and versatile candidate." [64] The advice was well taken for the president's conduct during the campaign matches the above recommendations. Clifford had sensed what the American people wanted to see in a Democratic candidate, and like any excellent salesman he made his product as marketable as possible. In many respects his appraisal of the kind of public image a chief executive needed foreshadowed the present concern for the image a candidate must have in order to be elected.

The last two items to be discussed in the political section were "Foreign Policy" and the president as "The Commander-in-Chief." [65] In the area of foreign policy, Truman's image had to be one of leader of the country. While acknowledging that there might be some merit in having Secretary of State George C. Marshall considered the country's "spokesman" on foreign policy, Clifford argued that this idea should be avoided because it made for "bad politics" for the election.[66] The president had to place himself in a situation where he could receive recognition for making foreign policy decisions that the people applauded.[67] As Clifford had said earlier, politics in 1948 was going to be more important than bipartisan foreign policy. Mr. Truman had to use his office to make certain that the political rewards for maintaining a tough line toward Russia and implementing the Marshall Plan did not slip through his fingers. In fact, Clifford reminded the president of the following thought: "In the American Republic, *the President is responsible* for foreign policy. He cannot be responsible in fact if he cannot use his authority. It is on *his* record, not that of Marshall, that the people will make their judgment in 1948, and he must be given the credit if he is subject to the blame. Democratic Government means no less and no more than that." [68] This realistic statement is difficult to contradict. A president takes the credit and the criticism for the actions of his administration. Closer analysis, however, reinforces the notion that there is an inextricable link, as the president's special counsel had already pointed out, between foreign and domestic policy. The president had to be prepared to capitalize on the popularity of the cold war, which he helped to bring about. On the issue of Truman as commander-in-chief, the memo argued that many statements regarding military matters could be made from the White House.[69] The American people had to be reminded that Harry Truman was their commander-in-chief as well as their president.

The last part of the memorandum was concerned with the program level. Clifford began by stating that the Democrats had to stay to the "left" of the Republicans in terms of strategy. He further maintained that the president was in a much better position than the Congress because he could act in a swifter fashion and with more frequency than that group.[70] Clifford also felt that the president could use the State of the Union Message to great advantage by presenting his program in it. "There is little possibility that he will get much cooperation from the Congress but we want the President to be in a position to receive the credit for whatever they do accomplish while also being in position to criticize the Congress for being obstructionists in failing to comply with other recommendations. This will be a fertile field for the development of campaign issues." [71] These words were prophetic beyond anybody's greatest expectations. Truman would hammer away at the Eightieth Congress in an extraordinarily effective way in 1948. In terms of concrete issues, Clifford named "(1) High Prices; (2) Housing; (3) The Marshall Plan; (4) Tax Revision; (5) Conservation of Natural Resources in the West; and (6) Civil Rights" as the most important ones for the campaign.[72]

On the problem of high prices, it was argued that the Truman administration had pushed for a "bold program" that would have "great appeal." [73] Concerning housing, Clifford urged that the administration take a strong stand. "Housing should be stressed in the State of the Union Message but its importance is such that a special message should go to the Congress on Housing shortly after the State of the Union Message has been delivered." [74] Truman did, in fact, follow these suggestions. The issue was included in the State of the Union Message and a special message was sent to Congress on February 23, 1948. According to Professor Richard O. Davies, the president had become the leading national advocate of housing reform by mid-March 1948.[75] For Clifford this strategy was perfect; Truman could only win votes because of his housing stand.

Turning to the Marshall Plan, Clifford speculated that it would be passed by the Congress because there was a great need for it.[76] This passage, of course, would be of great benefit to the president in the election year. On tax revision, Clifford recommended that the Democrats reap the political harvest from a tax cut. He advised that a message be sent to Congress in January calling for a revision of the existing tax structure.[77] It was his opinion that Truman could only gain from such a move. "If the Congress accepted the President's recommendations and passed such a tax bill, then there would be a division of credit. If the Congress refused to heed the President's suggestions and passed a bill allowing a much larger tax reduction, particularly for the higher income groups, then the administration would have another valuable issue to present in November of 1948." [78] The shrewdness of this move is obvious. Clifford was charting a course that would spell disaster for the president's political foes.

Conservation, the fifth of the key issues, proved very significant in the West. Clifford asked that an "imaginative" pro-

gram be put forth with 1960 as its target date. This kind of
step could "kill off the Wallaces and the demagogues who will
come after him. More practically, it will mean money in the
political bank in November 1948." [79] He then discussed the
all-important black vote explaining that the Republicans
were doing everything they could to win back this electorate.[80] He predicted that the Republicans would "offer an
FEPC, an anti-poll tax bill, and an anti-lynching bill" in the
next Congressional session.[81] To counter, the president had to
push for whatever action he felt necessary "to protect the
rights of minority groups." Although the South might not
like this action, it was the "lesser of two evils." [82]

The final part of the memorandum dealt with *"The Me-
chanics for 1948."* Clifford recommended the establishment
of a "small 'working committee' (or 'think' group)" to act as
a coordinating agent for the administration.[83] The men in
this group would be "close-mouthed," creative Truman supporters with an understanding of the workings of government
and politics.[84] This body would involve itself with working
on the Democratic platform, gathering material for the
president's major speeches, and presenting Truman with a
"monthly estimate" of the political situation.[85] The group
was also to have experts to deal with the candidates involved
in the election. The experts' main concern would be to find
weaknesses in an individual's record. The three names mentioned in this regard were Dewey, Robert Taft, and Truman.
(Truman was included so that the Democrats would be able
to counter any attacks on him.) While Wallace's name was
not mentioned here, someone was later employed to act as
a source on him.[86] This group was also to provide material
to Democrats for answering Republican attacks on the administration.[87]

Clifford concluded his analysis with dedicated and optimistic words: "No effort must be overlooked or left undone
to furnish President Truman with the greatest possible assistance because the future of this country and future of the
world are linked inextricably with his reelection. . . . If the

program discussed here can be put into operation soon and executed properly, it can help in persuading the American people to make up their minds the *right way.*" [88] The president's special counsel had examined the issues of the day and found the Republicans to be the major enemy. To be sure, Henry Wallace was discussed and a strategy was presented to offset his influence. However, in the total picture, the forecast of a third party would play a minor role in influencing what Truman would do. In overall strategy, even when the president was instructed to move left, he was advised to move with the Republican party as his guideline and not the Wallace group. Next, we examine how the Democrats, including the president, responded when Wallace made his announcement to run.

IV

REACTION

On December 29, 1947, San Francisco District Attorney Edmund G. (Pat) Brown wrote to Presidential Secretary Matthew Connelly explaining that the political situation in California looked good for Mr. Truman. There were problems in the state organization, but they could be corrected, thereby setting the stage for the president to carry the state.[1] The primary importance of Brown's optimistic letter, however, is the *date* it was written, for on the evening of the 29th, Henry Wallace announced his candidacy on a third party ticket. While Brown's views probably brought some comfort to the administration, most Democrats and political reporters were concerned with assessing the possible impact of the Wallace candidacy. At the time, comments on the action were offered by newspapers, magazines, and prominent individuals from both major parties. And in February the election of a Wallace-supported Congressional candidate in the Bronx led to more speculation about the possible consequences of the Wallace campaign. This chapter surveys some of the various assessments offered at the time on the probable effect of the Wallaceites upon the election.

Wallace attacked both major parties in his declaration of candidacy,[2] but even the left-leaning *Nation* Magazine as of December 27, 1947, was certain that a third party would mean victory for the Republicans.[3] And as early as July 1947, Wilson Wyatt, national chairman of the Americans for Democratic Action had said that such a move "would be a catastrophe" to liberals and progressives generally.[4] Prospects for the Democrats looked dismal at the beginning of 1948.

In a December 18, 1947, editorial in *PM,* Max Lerner explained that a Wallace candidacy would be of great benefit to the Republicans, and for this reason he was strongly opposed to a new party. "A third party without a phantom of a chance to win makes no sense," argued Lerner.[5] On the day following the former vice-president's radio broadcast, Lerner editorialized in *PM* that his paper's position had not changed from its earlier one. "PM's position is still what it was. We still think that a Third Party in the field in 1948 is a mistaken move, based on mistaken premises, and likely to do great harm not only to the Democrats, but to the independent progressive forces as well." [6] Lerner continued by saying that the Wallace group lacked a substantial base and that the movement was not "synonymous" with "American independent progressivism." Lerner also felt compelled to point out that Communists were involved in the new party, which did not speak well for it.[7] To a liberal journalist like Max Lerner, then, support for the Wallace movement was out, and he thought that Wallace probably spelled doom for the Democrats.

The *New York Times* also had editorial reaction to Wallace's announcement. The newspaper was critical, as its editorial explained: "He is ready to run for President on a third ticket, and he is not deterred by the thought that this action may chiefly injure the party which twice honored him with Cabinet Office and once elected him to the Vice Presidency." [8] To these observations may be added those of *Nation* magazine. In its January 3 edition, *Nation* lamented the fact that Wallace felt it necessary to abandon his fight within the Democratic party. On January 10, Freda Kirchway stated that *Nation* believed Wallace's action to be strategically unwise. She explained that liberal attacks on the administration were now tempered due to fear of association with the third party.[9] Not even the very progressive *Nation* could support the new party venture.

On December 29, the *Washington Post* wrote about Wallace: "Even if he is willing to sacrifice himself in order to defeat Mr. Truman, he must now realize that the sorry spectacle he is making of himself may redound to the President's advantage." [10] In the long run this possibility proved true, but most observers did not see it at the time. Curtis MacDougall has reported that David Lawrence and Ralph McGill were the only two "nationally prominent columnists" he knew of that took this view.[11] On January 4, 1948, the *Post* carried a column written by Edward Folliard entitled, "Somebody Errs About Gideon's Army." [12] The column summarized various newspaper reactions to the Wallace candidacy. For example, the *New York Herald Tribune* felt that Wallace would drain votes from every party, but that he would "not be the potent figure he considers himself!" while the *New York Mirror* maintained that "Such a split would spell a Republican victory in 1948, except that the Republicans have a crack which may develop into a crevasse. The crack is over . . . the Marshall Plan." The *St. Paul Pioneer Press* claimed that Wallace had opened the door for a Republican victory that would be in opposition to everything he stands for. "He may well be making sure that reaction will be enthroned at home for the next four years and that war with Russia becomes inevitable."

In contrast to the opinion put forth by the *Pioneer Press* and other forecasters who predicted doom for the Democrats, a sampling of Southern newspapers by Folliard indicates that they had different notions. The *Mobile Register* claimed that Wallace "represents nothing but a washed up, disgruntled New Deal politician with a confusion of fantastic theories and a glib tongue." *The Montgomery Advertiser* used the term "good riddance" to sum up its feelings on the action, and in Tennessee the *Nashville Tennesseean* said that "Henry Wallace as an announced candidate has lost his mysterious charm. He is now very small potatoes." In North Carolina the *Raleigh News and Observer* said that "The liberals of this country have too much at stake in the next four years to be willing to cast a protest vote that would be in effect a vote for a Republican President," while Ralph McGill's *Atlanta Constitution* said Wallace would have no effect on Truman's defeat or victory. Most of the Southern papers would be influenced by Wallace's civil rights stand but even the *Raleigh News and Observer* and the *Atlanta Constitution* saw the Wallace candidacy as something less than a hindrance to Harry Truman's election.

Despite the fact that some newspapers felt that Wallace's impact would be minimal, some people, especially in the Republican party, felt very confident about a Republican presidential victory in 1948. Representative Clarence Brown of Ohio for one predicted that a Republican victory was a certainty because of the Wallace candidacy.[13] According to columnist Folliard, most Republicans believed that the third party would aid their cause, but there were some who were unsure of how great its impact would be. For example, Indiana's Charles Halleck, Republican House majority leader was quoted as saying, "This is as good a time as any to find out how much strength Mr. Wallace has in the country. His being a candidate will clarify things. It's awfully hard to tell what the effect will be on the 1948 elections." [14] But even though some members of the GOP were uncertain about the long run effects of the candidacy, jubilation and confidence appear to be the more typical Republican reactions.

Of course, Democrats also reacted to Wallace's announcement. Mr. Truman, however, chose to remain silent on the matter. In his news conference of December 31, the president was asked about the possible consequences of the Wallace move and chose to answer with a "No comment on that." [15] From this action one can surmise that Truman was adhering to the Clifford suggestion that individuals other than the president attack the former vice-president. In fact, Truman himself seldom mentioned the third party during the campaign year, but he was in contact with those who did. On the day Wallace announced his candidacy, New York's Senator Robert F. Wagner responded with a statement of his own. In part it said,

> American people, the Democratic Party or the Republican Party—none of them are war mongers. I think the Democratic Administration is following the only, if dif-

ficult, path to peace. Certainly the Democratic Party
and I, as a member of that Party, have fought successfully to extend political, economic and social democracy.
Under President Truman's leadership we shall see that
fight through, and we won't have to resort to revolutionary methods, but shall achieve concretely and demo-
cratically the goals to which Henry Wallace refers.

Yes, the angels are weeping and there is a great man
and good friend of Henry Wallace who, I am sure,
weeps with them.

Truman thanked Wagner on January 5, saying that he
thought he had issued a "good statement," [16] but that expression was the extent of what he was saying about Wallace
for the time being.

Democratic Congressman John McCormack of Massachusetts, then minority whip, was quoted as saying that the action would aid the party. In the long run his comment
seems to have been quite perceptive even if it seemed like
mere rhetoric at the time. "Wallace will be in the position
of being supported openly by the Communist Party. . . .
The votes we may lose will be more than offset by those
voters who will support the Democratic Party because of
Wallace's attempt to create confusion." [17] Senator Scott Lucas
of Illinois was another Democrat who did not publically
think that Wallace would pose a threat. He expressed this
view by proclaiming that the new candidate "won't get
enough votes to wad a shotgun." [18] *Time* Magazine pointed
out that some Democrats now believed that Truman was going to benefit from the candidacy because of Wallace's Communist support.[19] The taint of "red support" would no longer
be connected with the Democrats.

One of the men who blasted Wallace's actions was Rhode
Island Senator J. Howard McGrath, chairman of the Democratic National Committee. In the January 3 edition of *Capital Comment,* a publication of the Democratic National
Committee, some of McGrath's statements regarding Wallace
were excerpted. The Rhode Island senator maintained that

"Wallace will not attract true liberals . . . because liberals understand . . . that a third party movement . . . will serve only to assist the forces of reaction." McGrath also linked Wallace to the Communists saying "that a vote for Wallace . . . is a vote for the things for which Stalin, Molotov, and Vishinsky stand." [20] Following these remarks came *Capital Comment*'s conclusion.

> Major danger in the Wallace campaign is that it will obscure the fact that the voter has three choices in 1948:
> (1) *To throw away his vote on Wallace.*
> (2) *To vote for Republican reaction and four years of Taftwit bumbling.*
> (3) *To vote for President Truman and a Democratic Program of true progressive liberalism to go into effect on January 1, 1949.* [21]

Thus, at the very outset of the campaign, important Democrats were lashing out at Wallace, identifying him with the Communists, and an organ of the party was publicizing McGrath's harsh attack.

An appraisal of the initial impact of the Wallace announcement was also made by Frank McNaughton. McNaughton was Washington correspondent for *Time* from 1941 to 1949 and was also a coauthor of two books on Truman published in 1945 and 1948, respectively. Dated January 2, 1948, McNaughton's assessment explained that there were various interpretations of what the Wallace candidacy would do to the Democratic party. He said, however, that Democrats felt that the bolt would not do much damage and might in the long run even help the president. [22] McNaughton also pointed out that many Democrats felt "that Wallace plus Communist support" would pull conservative Democrats back to the fold. [23] In his analysis of possible support, the journalist said that some Republicans were expecting Wallace to get about three hundred thousand ballots in New York. However, some Republicans like Joe Martin were unsure about that specific point. McNaughton also claimed that Wallace would be strong in Connecticut and possibly in California. In the Midwest the Democrats were going to gain because of Wallace, for it was thought that he would draw "Republican isolationists' votes." [24] So far as the Negro vote was concerned, it was argued that a large Wallace inroad in the cities would aid the Democrats because blacks had been returning to the GOP.[25] This statement lends credence to Clark Clifford's contention that Republicans were the people to fear with respect to the black vote.

McNaughton completed his remarks with a characterization of the situation as it then existed. His first observation was that as of January 1, the Wallace candidacy was of no help to Truman and in fact might cause damage in New York, California, and Chicago. His second observation came to the heart of the matter: "By the time Wallace has taken a campaign hammering, and the GOP has had Wallace and Communism tied around its neck, it is quite possible that Wallace will not cut as much third party ice as first glances would indicate. It is doubtful that he can long survive a campaign slogan that 'A vote for Wallace is a vote for Stalin,' and that's what the Democrats intend to pin on him." [26] McNaughton's forecast was accurate, and it coincided with the strategy set forth in the Clifford memo. From the beginning of the election year, although Democrats were concerned about Wallace, they thought they had a way of successfully countering his candidacy, and they were correct.

In February, a Congressional election was held in New York city's (Bronx) Twenty-fourth District to fill a vacancy, and the results of this election turned out to be the high point of the Progressive campaign.[27] The position was contested by four candidates: Leo Isacson of the American Labor party who was endorsed and supported by Wallace; Karl Propper, the Democrat; Dean Alfange, the Liberal party candidate; and Joseph DeNigris, the Republican contender. Many claimed that this election would be an excellent test of strength for Wallace's forces. The *Herald Tribune,* for example, had the following to say on the day the election was held:

> If there is indeed third-party fright in the White House, today is important. . . . This is a full-fledged test, four parties in the race, and the big question is: How strong is Henry Wallace? The full Wallace force is behind the American Labor Party candidate, Assemblyman Leo Isacson. Today's election has far-reaching significance. . . . If his man, Mr. Isacson, shows marked strength, the third party has something to crow about, for then Henry Wallace might hold the balance of power in this state next November. In any event, we should see today a clear-cut demonstration of Mr. Wallace's attraction for the "common man" of whom he is forever speaking, plus an indication of what the hard Communist organizational core can do for a candidate. This is an election for the nation to watch.[28]

The district, however, as Alonzo Hamby has correctly pointed out, had certain characteristics that made it politically peculiar and difficult to generalize about. The Twenty-fourth usually gave the American Labor party a high vote; it had a substantial Jewish population; and its Democrats would not cooperate with its Liberals.[29] Despite the fact that the Twenty-fourth was special in many ways, *Nation* referred to the upcoming election as "The first test of strength for the American Labor Party since the Amalgamated Clothing Workers walked out over the Wallace issue." [30] However, the magazine did alert its readers to the point that an Isacson election might not be as important as it seemed. Discussing the Democratic-Liberal disharmony in the district, the journal concluded: "In effect, this means that to gauge President Truman's strength in the district, as opposed to Wallace's, one will have to add the Alfange vote to the Propper vote. It is well to allow too, for the fact that the Twenty-fourth is the A.L.P.'s second strongest district; its sentiments should not be considered typical of those in Massachusetts, Idaho, or for that matter, most of New York." [31] Yet, no matter what anybody cautioned before the election, it appeared a showdown of sorts.

On February 15 Wallace came to the Bronx and delivered a speech before some eighty-five hundred people.[32] When the votes of the February 17 election were counted, Isacson had won a tremendous victory polling 22,697 votes while the combined total of the three other candidates came to a little less than 18,000.[33] The Wallace people were elated with the results, while Democrats and Liberals were distressed. Wallace was quoted as saying that the election was "a repudiation of the get-tough, double-standard foreign policy that has been leading us toward war." [34] Shortly after the election Senator Glen Taylor of Idaho lent his name to the new party, saying that he would run as Wallace's vice-presidential candidate.[35]

Democrats tried so hard to explain what happened in the Bronx that *Time* Magazine noted that "Democratic alibis piled up thicker than mites on a slab of old store cheese." [36] *Time* acknowledged that it was a "special case," but even so, a Democratic defeat had indeed taken place, Edward Flynn, Democratic leader in the Bronx, who was supposed to make certain that upsets like this did not occur, explained that "the Communist menace to this country is much greater than most people thought." [37] Democratic National Chairman J. Howard McGrath also had a comment on the election: "The fight against Communism on the left and Toryism on the right cannot be won unless every Democrat resolves to get out and vote." [38] Eleanor Roosevelt, however, took another tack in her assessment of the situation. She spoke of "inflation and the fear of war" as the two principal issues that Wallace was speaking to in his campaign, and how effective these issues were with the voters.[39] The former first lady also spoke of the importance of the Palestine issue in gathering support for the ALP candidate. She concluded her thoughts with the following comments:

I do not agree with Edward J. Flynn, head of the Bronx Democratic organization, that the election is a revelation of the strength of the Communists which we did not recognize before. They were there before. They haven't greatly increased, but they could throw their full strength into this particular area because they had fertile ground in which to sow their seed.

I would say that this election points up a very simple thing—namely, that the Republicans and Democrats alike had better bestir themselves to remove the people's two great anxieties, or the course of our government in the next few years may be surprising to both parties.[40]

Other prominent people were also appraising what had happened. John McCormack explained that he did not think that the election indicated a national trend, while Chester Bowles hoped that the Isacson victory would benefit the Democrats by waking them up.[41] Wilson Wyatt concluded that the Democrats suffered from a light vote and that the party had to get out a heavy vote in November if it expected victory.[42] One of the most scathing comments came from Max Lerner in a front-page editorial entitled "The Lesson of the Isacson Victory": "The overwhelming Isacson victory in the Bronx Congressional race was, without question a Wallace victory as well. . . . This ought to be something for President Truman and the Democratic leaders to chew over—and Henry Wallace as well. The first move is up to the Democrats. Either they must change their cynical and bungling policies, or they must change their Presidential candidate." [43] A day before the Lerner editorial appeared, Warren Moscow of the *New York Times* had also concluded that the Wallace party had engineered "an upset with national political connotations." [44] Certainly this was not a joyous time for the Democratic leaders who had to read the various analyses of the election and speak about the causes of the Democratic loss.

All, however, was not as bad as it seemed on the surface. One of the most astute analyses of the election came from Gus Tyler, political director of the International Ladies' Garment Workers' Union. Tyler's memorandum, which was presented to the Americans for Democratic Action, carefully examined the election using a 1946 East Side special election for comparative purposes.[45] Tyler's conclusions disagreed with the prevailing sentiment. He argued that the election failed to demonstrate a "Wallace trend" and that the Democratic candidate "might have won" if Ed Flynn had cooperated with the Liberal party and if "the Administration had pursued a strong pro-Palestine policy."[46] Also, according to Tyler, the Communist party had done excellent organizational work for Isacson and it had paid off. "I think it proves the power of pure organization in winning elections," was the last remark of the memo.[47] Judged by later events, Mr. Tyler's cogent thoughts proved most accurate in describing the situation.

The president remained silent about the election, but on February 23, Howard McGrath had more comment on the Wallace candidacy. McGrath said that Wallace could "defeat . . . the Democratic Party's program of practical liberalism in 1948."[48] According to the newspaper clipping from which the statement was taken, it followed a McGrath remark calling the Isacson election a "danger sign" for the Democratic party. This comment by itself would seem to indicate that some Democrats had begun to be very apprehensive about Wallace. And that indication was probably true, for the headline concerning the McGrath story was "McGrath Admits Peril to Party, Pleads with Wallace to Stop Drive."[49] However, along with anxieties came the necessity to associate Wallace with the Communists. "The fact that the loudest applause for Henry Wallace comes from Communists, Communist fellow-travelers and reactionary Republicans causes me to believe that the bulk of Henry Wallace's support is coming from those whose allegiance is not to the American way of life."[50] Remarks like this one and others like the one made by Edward Flynn forced the public to think about the role of the Communist party in the Wallace movement. Such was the political strategy being followed.

The issue of Communist activity had also been directly injected into the February 17 election. On February 10, Liberal candidate Dean Alfange had sent Henry Wallace a telegram in which he charged Isacson with being the recipient of Communist support.[51] Since Isacson was heartily endorsed by Wallace, this charge was against Wallace as well. On the day before the election, over WQXR, Alfange charged that "the Communist party has mobilized its entire manpower, and has thrown its entire strength into that district." [52] A. A. Berle, head of New York's Liberal party also took part in the action. In a February 15 radio broadcast over WMCA he attacked Wallace and the American Labor party as being supported by Communists.[53] Calling Wallace "a . . . front for international intrigue," he also spoke of the former vice-president as an appeaser of Russia, and informed his listeners that there was no faster way to war than to follow Wallace's proposals.[54] It is improbable that the Democratic party had influenced prominent Liberal party members to take such a staunch anti-Communist line, especially since the two organizations were working against each other in that election, but the actions of Berle and Alfange fitted precisely into the strategy that the Democrats were employing against the Wallace candidacy.

Harry Truman had remained very reserved about Henry Wallace's candidacy from the announcement until March 17, 1948. In his January 22, 1948, news conference, Mr. Truman maintained that a candidate would have a better chance of winning were he in one of the major parties rather than in a third party, but there was no reference to Wallace by name.[55] However, on St. Patrick's Day, in New York City, the president spoke out in the most forceful of terms. Addressing the Friendly Sons of St. Patrick in a late evening speech that was carried across the country by radio, Truman impressed his audience by saying: "I do not want and I will not accept the political support of Henry Wallace and his Communists. If joining them or permitting them to join me is the price of victory, I recommend defeat. These are days of high prices for everything, but any price for Wallace and his Communists is too much for me to pay. I'm not buying." [56] Truman added these words to the text of the address he was supposed to give.[57] However, his remarks were not as extemporaneous as they might have appeared. On March 5, George Elsey sent Clark Clifford a memorandum concerning the president's upcoming speech of March 17. Elsey proposed that the speech deal with "Russian relations." [58] He further argued that it be broken into four parts, the second part being relevant to Wallace. *"Part B:* A rejection, with full explanation, of the prevailing current fallacy which Henry Wallace is advocating so eloquently that a meeting between the President and Stalin is the answer to our current problems. (This would be big headline news.)" [59] The president gave two addresses on March 17. In his speech to Congress he discussed Russian relations and requested fast implementation of the Marshall Plan, universal military training, and the "temporary reenactment of selective service legislation." [60] Truman here omitted any reference to Wallace.

In his talk to the Friendly Sons of St. Patrick, Truman obviously felt that the time was right for him to openly attack the left. His remarks were certain to strike responsive chords in a Catholic organization. Wallace had blamed the United States for the Russian take-over of Czechoslovakia in February. In a Minneapolis speech of February 27, he explained:

> Let's use our heads—not just the headlines. What is happening in Czechoslovakia is not just a tempest in a vacuum. There is a very clear pattern of cause and effect—a triangular pattern connecting Moscow, Prague and Washington. Every act under the Truman Doctrine is clearly labelled—"Anti-Russian." The men in Moscow would, *from their viewpoint,* be utter morons if they failed to respond with acts of *pro-Russian* consoli-

dation. The Czechoslovakia story will repeat itself so long as our gun and dollar policies in Greece, in China, and elsewhere on Russia's doorstep are continued. Only peace with Russia will stop the march toward war.[61]

In early March Wallace expanded on his earlier remarks and also alleged that United States Ambassador Laurence Steinhardt was in some part responsible for the Czech coup because he had prepared a statement that served to help the Rightists in the country and thus bring about the crisis.[62] Wallace was in a very vulnerable position, and the president probably surmised that this was the perfect opportunity to blast him and make the third party politically ineffective. And the thought of discussing Wallace within part of a major speech had already been brought up by Clifford's assistant.

The overall effect of Truman's attack is difficult to ascertain. The *Washington Post,* in an editorial, was critical because it felt that the president was driving off liberal support.[63] On the other hand, the cheers that greeted the president's comment might have been indicative of the general reaction that was felt after the speech.[64] Wallace himself answered Truman in a number of radio broadcasts. On March 19 he said, "When he attempted to brand as 'Communists' those who support our fight for peace, Mr. Truman appealed to prejudice, because he could not answer us with reason." [65] A week later on NBC radio, the former vice-president included the following in his speech:

> The men who speak of reigns of terror in Europe are fast introducing a reign of terror here at home. They are trying to silence all opposition to their program of regimentation and preparation for war by intimidation, threats, and by using every available means to frighten the people into silence.
>
> I tell you that the greatest threat to American freedom today comes from within our own country.
>
> President Truman set the pattern when he branded the millions who oppose his policies as "communists."

> Such an appeal to prejudice blots out reason and un-
> leashes dangerous forces of hate that threaten the free-
> dom and livelihood of all Americans.[66]

Obviously Wallace was angry, and knew that he had to
counter the president's charges if he had any hopes of keeping his campaign in high gear. Actually, however, if the polls
were any indication, February was a good month for the
third party: it was estimated then that it would get a fair
share of the vote.[67]

On March 19 Frank McNaughton issued another appraisal
of the situation which seems to have been accurate.[68] Mc-
Naughton claimed that most Democrats believed that Wallace had lost some of his punch because of his intemperate
speeches. However, Wallace still had to be considered a
"serious threat" because he had the support of "the lunatic
fringe and the pacifists and Commies" which groups ac-
counted for a large number of votes.[69] According to Mc-
Naughton, Sam Rayburn and Howard McGrath both thought
that Truman benefited from his St. Patrick's Day comments
about Wallace and his emphasis on "Communism vs. Freedom." [70] Concluding the assessment, McNaughton pointed
out that Rayburn thought the idea of "hammering away" at
Communists would be beneficial to Truman.[71] Up to March
19, "Wallace was whittling at Truman and now the whittling is going both ways," said McNaughton in his last sentence.[72] It is interesting to note that the *Time* correspondent
had gone from a position on January 2 of relative calm, to
a position on March 19 of serious concern with regard to
assessing the possibilities of the Wallace impact. But the
pendulum would swing again, and the Democrats would become *relatively* unconcerned about the Wallace challenge.

By March 20 the Democrats were paying attention to the
Wallace candidacy but doing so in a cautious, calculating
way. On March 17 the president had publicly struck at Wallace and his connection with Communists for the first time.
This act crystallized the tough stand that the Democrats were
taking with respect to the third party. The Isacson victory

had certainly upset the Democrats, but, all factors considered, the party rebounded well. Its prestige had been damaged, but individuals were continuing in their attacks on the Communist support that Wallace was receiving, and even the president had joined in. Immediate press reaction to the Wallace candidacy had been mixed, but those publications that thought the move would benefit the Democrats would be proven correct. Many prominent Democrats also maintained that Wallace's move would benefit their party. Even if this idea was early campaign rhetoric, in the end it, too, proved to be correct. Also, by the middle of March, an important development had taken place: Truman had presented a number of proposals that indicated that he was moving in a more "liberal" direction—at least on paper. The Democratic party had moved into a much more advantageous position than the new party could ever hope to obtain.

V

ISSUES OF THE CAMPAIGN

If the conventional wisdom regarding the impact of third parties in the United States holds true, it should be possible to discern a shift within the Democratic party during the period when the Wallace Progressives challenged it. Henry Wallace, following the election, was apparently convinced that the third party had played its part in forcing the president to seek new directions. As the former vice-president wrote "The stronger the Progressive Party and the ALP, the greater the probability of the Democrats behaving themselves." [1] Indeed, Wallace's running mate in the ill-fated third party venture, the Idaho senator, Glen Taylor, as late as 1967 believed that the Trumanites stole the Progressive party's domestic program in 1948.[2] Former Florida Senator Claude Pepper also believes that the Progressives had an impact on Truman. In a 1953 interview he expressed the view that the Progressives may have pushed the Democratic party further left than Truman desired.[3] At the same interview he addressed himself to a question dealing with why the Progressive party failed in 1948. In his estimation, "The Progressive Party flopped for the same reason that all other third parties have in the U.S. When a third party starts up, one of the two major parties will lean far enough over to leave a very narrow fringe. One of the major parties leans or veers far enough over to satisfy most of the discontented." [4] With respect to the 1948 election, this kind of reasoning is unsound. An analysis of the issues raised by the Democrats shows that the party stood absolutely firm on foreign policy and if it did move at all domestically, it was primarily because of the Republicans.

Walter LaFeber, however, believes that the Progressives were able to make foreign policy an issue in the campaign, though he does not write that Truman changed positions because of the third party.[5] Two other accounts are more on target. In the first, Paul Hammond explains that "Foreign-policy issues, ironically, had little impact on the conduct of the 1948 campaign or the electoral verdict. . . . Henry Wallace's campaign as the Progressive-party candidate for president attempted but failed to raise the saliency of foreign-policy issues for the 1948 electorate." [6] In the second, Richard Kirkendall declares that "Although Wallace did stimulate some discussion of foreign policy by other campaigners he did not make it the dominant issue as he hoped to do." [7] There were a myriad of reasons for this failure. Wallace's extreme charges concerning the coup in Czechoslovakia, coupled with Soviet actions in Berlin explain the reluctance of many people to back the third party; charges of Communist infiltration in the movement provide further explanation. In addition, Truman very wisely decided to refuse to engage in a public debate on foreign policy while emphasizing his positive accomplishments in this area. Finally, and perhaps most important was the fact that the voters had an issue much closer to home to focus upon: the Eightieth Congress. Foreign policy was remote to most voters, and it was a subject that the chief executive had more information about than any other American, for decision-making purposes. But high prices, lack of adequate housing, civil rights, farm policy, repeal of Taft-Hartley, and minimum wage and social security increases were the kinds of gut-level issues that aroused the people. Tactically, foreign policy had been a poor issue on which to found a new party, but the Progressives were dedicated to restructuring the nation's policy. In the end, though, the Progressives failed to pull Truman or the Democrats in its direction on foreign affairs.[8]

As a presidential candidate, Henry Wallace had to find ways of making his positions clear to the electorate. One such opportunity presented itself when an officer of a United Automobile Workers Union local requested that Wallace spell out his political views. On domestic policy, Wallace explained that he had not altered his views since 1944.[9] Essentially, he argued for a traditional, liberal approach to domestic problems including repeal of the Taft-Hartley Act in the 1948 election year.[10]

Foreign policy, however, was the crucial issue for Wallace, and he had a chance to come to grips with it when the following question was posed by the union official: "We are worried about war. How do you propose to prevent it?"

> I think we can prevent war and build world peace if we take the conduct of our domestic and foreign policy away from the militarists and bankers now in control in Washington. Once this is done it would be possible, in terms of the Roosevelt policy of building peace through the United Nations. . . . I believe furthermore that the record of the war and postwar relations shows that cooperation between the United States and the USSR is possible. My program rests on this record and on the thesis that fair and equal cooperation is not only possible but necessary for world peace and prosperity. I would shift from our present bi-partisan policy of cold war and civil war today and atomic war tomorrow to a policy of progressive disarmament and friendly relations among all the nations of the world. . . .
>
> At home, I think we must put an end to the war hysteria and war preparation. I am opposed to the giant war budget for militarizing America. I oppose compulsory military service in peacetime whether it is in the form of a draft or universal military training.[11]

Thus Wallace had enunciated the heart of his program: a world based on coexistence rather than arms races. Many critics would be quick to point out that this program was not practical enough, but to Henry Wallace the above words spelled out a world in which capitalism and communism thrived side by side.

Wallace's letter continued by citing the names of men

from the military and "Wall Street" who held important positions in government. He then presented his views on ending monopoly in America, stated his conviction for government ownership of the nation's aircraft corporations ("I favor public ownership of the aircraft industry because this industry is helping foment the present war hysteria in order to profiteer from war contracts"), and tackled the charges that the Communist party was responsible for the formation of the third party. "Any Communist who supports the independent ticket will be supporting our program not the Communist program. I am not a Communist, Socialist or Marxist of any description but I find nothing criminal in the advocacy of differing economic and social ideas, however much I differ with them." [12] While there was much logic to Wallace's argument it was unconvincing to the great majority of voters.

The new party's positions were also stated, among other places, in a " 'Canned' Speech" entitled, "Why Third Party." [13] The speech began with an indictment of the two-party system, claiming that both parties were monopoly controlled.[14] A brief history of party development in the United States followed in an attempt to legitimize the formation of the new party. "New parties arise in a time of crisis when the old parties are no longer run in the interests of the majority of the nation. This is such a time of crisis." [15] The Progressives then focused on the Democratic party, which, according to them, bore "no resemblance to the great coalition led by FDR. It has deserted the people. 'I didn't leave the Democratic Party,' Glen Taylor said when he decided to run for vice president on the new party ticket; 'The Democratic party left me.' " [16] This was an important charge since part of the Progressive strategy was to link itself to FDR's past glories. As former vice-president under the deceased president, Wallace certainly had the credentials to hammer away at this theme. The Progressives also attacked what they considered the "bi-partisan" nature of the Democratic party. Calling the Democrats "practically indistinguishable from the Republican party," [17] the speech singled out areas where bipartisanship was doing great harm to the country. Bipartisanship in inflation, farm policy, civil rights, and foreign policy was causing the nation to deviate from the Rooseveltian path. The statement on foreign policy is a key one with respect to the party's charges. "A bi-partisan foreign policy is strangling the United Nations, restoring Nazis to power in Germany, suppressing the democratic aims of peoples all over the world, handcuffing war-torn nations to Wall Street and demanding compulsory military training and the draft in preparation for World War III." [18]

An attack on Harry Truman followed. According to the Progressives the president was guilty of driving New Dealers from the government and replacing them with men having no sympathy for the common man.[19] Truman was also accused of being hostile to labor—so hostile in fact that he was charged with "strike-breaking and labor-baiting." Truman's Taft-Hartley veto was explained away by quoting from former New Dealer Harold Ickes who maintained that "The evidence is clear that Truman wanted to have a chance to veto the Taft-Hartley bill, but he also wanted the law passed over his veto." [20] Despite what the Progressives charged, the Taft-Hartley veto had come over loud and clear to labor; to argue that the president had been insincere in the action was rather foolhardy on their part, for he had vehemently denounced the bill.

The Progressives also criticized what they considered the illusion of the "liberal" Democratic party. They pointed out, quite correctly, that there was no chance of gaining control of the Democratic National Convention.[21] For the Progressives the only choice was Wallace and Taylor leading a "New Party." The final segment of the speech again linked Wallace with Roosevelt hoping to draw upon the New Deal image. "Four times in a row the American people voted for the program which Wallace alone represents today." [22] It was only through a large Wallace vote, said the Progressives, that the party could look forward to growth in the years to come.

The 1948 Progressive party platform provides another source for viewing the party's stands. This document also accused both major political parties of having been captured by "Big Business." "Today . . . private power has constituted itself an invisible government which pulls the strings of its puppet Republican and Democratic parties. Two sets of candidates compete for votes under the outworn emblems of the old parties. But both represent a single program—a program of monopoly profits through war reparations, lower living standards, and suppression of dissent." [23] The Progressives claimed to be "political heirs" of Lincoln, La Follette, and Franklin Roosevelt among others.[24] The attachment to FDR was obviously crucial and was used whenever possible.

The Wallaceites indicted the "old parties" for betraying the American people. The platform argued that neither party wanted real peace: "The American people want peace. But the old parties, obedient to the dictates of monopoly and the military, prepare for war in the name of peace. They refuse to negotiate a settlement of differences with the Soviet Union." [25] The major parties, in the eyes of the Progressives, were also guilty of failing to use the United Nations as a body for promoting peace, and using the Marshall Plan for the rebuilding of "Nazi Germany." [26] The platform also blasted the Democrats and Republicans for supporting the Truman Doctrine saying, "They finance and arm corrupt, fascist governments in China, Greece, Turkey, and elsewhere through the Truman Doctrine, wasting billions of American resources and squandering America's heritage as the enemy of despotism." [27] This initial attack on foreign policy was concluded by explaining that "Peace cannot be won—but profits can—by spending ever increasing billions of the people's money in war preparations." [28]

"Peace, freedom, and abundance," were the principles that the Progressive party was founded upon, but the focus of the Progressive drive was on the peace issue. The party's general position on foreign policy is illustrated in the following words extracted from the "Principles" section of the platform. "The Progressive Party holds that basic to the organization of world peace is a return to the purpose of Franklin Roosevelt to seek areas of international agreement rather than disagreement. It was his conviction that within the United Nations different social and economic systems can and must live together. If peace is to be achieved capitalistic United States and communist Russia must establish good relations and work together." [29] Freedom and abundance were the terms the Progressives used to describe their domestic program.[30] That program constituted an attack on discrimination in America, including anti-Communist discrimination through loyalty oaths, and constituted a belief that the "people" had to control the economy. The most important aspect of the program, however, was peace. "The Progressive Party believes that only through peaceful understanding can the world make progress toward reconstruction and higher standards of living; that peace is the essential condition for safeguarding and extending our traditional freedoms; that only by preserving liberty and by planning an abundant life for all can we eliminate the sources of world conflict. Peace, freedom, and abundance—the goals of the Progressive Party—are indivisible." [31]

How did the Democrats choose to respond to the Progressive party position in 1948? At the outset of the election year, the Democratic party was presented with a unique chance for setting forth its position. Clark Clifford, in his memorandum that he recently called "an application of pure reason to politics," had recommended that the State of the Union Message serve as an announcement of the president's program for 1948, and indeed it did so serve.[32] On January 7, Harry Truman addressed a joint session of Congress and presented a message having a very broad scope. "Our first goal is to secure fully the essential human rights of our citizens," declared the president.[33] Discrimination was not in keeping with American values, and Truman promised to send a message to Congress based on the report of the President's Committee on Civil Rights. The black voter would now have something tangible to expect from the administration. Whether or not Truman was totally committed to this course of action is a moot point, for the political temper of the time was such that he had to make a move that would keep black voters from shifting their allegiances.

"Our second goal," said the president, "is to protect and develop our human resources." [34] He was speaking of improvements in health, education, social security, and housing. The president was calling for extension of already existing practices while at the same time asking for new measures. He told Congress that "unemployment compensation, old age benefits, and survivor's benefits" should be extended and that the level of benefits should be raised. With regard to the housing shortage, the president recommended the continuation and strengthening of rent control as well as federally provided, low-income housing.[35] Truman went beyond existing practices in the field of health care when he requested "a national system of payment for medical care based on well-tried insurance principles. . . . Our ultimate aim must be a comprehensive insurance system to protect all our people equally against insecurity and ill health." [36] It seems unlikely that the president had any intention of pushing for such a program, but this concept made good campaign rhetoric certain to attract votes in the election year.[37] Equally pathbreaking was Truman's recommendation that the federal government provide funds for education.

The president's third goal for the nation focused on the conservation of natural resources. In this area Truman called for an expanded reclamation program as well as the continued building of dams. He concluded his remarks on this topic by saying that the country "can learn much from our Tennessee Valley experience. We should no longer delay in applying lessons of that vast undertaking to our other great river basins." [38]

Truman then shifted to economics. The country had to work to raise the standard of living, to keep the economic system healthy, and to make certain that goods were widely distributed. For the farmer the president recommended, among other things, the continuation of price supports, but he said that the system had to "be reexamined and modernized." For workers he recommended that the minimum wage be raised from forty cents to seventy-five cents per hour.[39]

The fifth goal of the national administration concerned foreign policy. Here the president promised continued support for the United Nations and expressed confidence in its ability to succeed. He also spoke of the country's commitment to the economic reconstruction of Europe. Truman then struck indirectly at critics of his foreign policy: "We are following a sound, constructive, and practical course in carrying out our determination to achieve peace.

"We are fighting poverty, hunger, and suffering.

"This leads to peace—not war.

"Above all else, we are striving to achieve a concord among the peoples of the world based upon the dignity of the individual and the brotherhood of man.

"This leads to peace—not war." [40] It is evident that the president was aiming at those accusing him of leading the country into World War III.

The last part of the address dealt with inflation. Having already delivered a ten-point program aimed at halting inflation (November 17, 1947), the president merely reaffirmed that it had to be stopped. He then recommended an item that had not been included in his ten points. His proposal was a tax credit of $40 for every taxpayer and an additional $40 credit for each dependent. Truman explained that while this program should be applicable to all taxpayers, it would be of most help to those of low-income brackets.[41]

Truman had taken Clifford's advice and used the State of the Union Message to clarify his positions. With the exception of his later blistering attacks on the Republicans in Congress, Truman's 1948 campaign was portended in the speech. The speech itself is subject to two interpretations. First, it was an election year. Even if the president had not been fully convinced by the suggestions of the Clifford memorandum, he at least seems to have been guided by it in his proposals to Congress. Of some import was the fact that there was little or no chance of passage of a national health insurance law. The president, as Clifford had advised, had to make his position clear to the voters of the country. Richard Davies writes of this action: "If the Republican Congress should have passed any of his programs, then he would have been able to tell the voters about his legislative triumphs; but if it turned down his suggestion, as seemed most likely, then he could blame the Republican leadership in the Congress. No matter what Congress did, therefore, Truman stood to reap the political harvest." [42] Journalist Irwin Ross, who has written the most recently published book on the 1948 election, has pointed out that the speech, if "viewed cynically," had an appeal to everybody. At the same time, it is also possible to conclude with Ross that the speech was more than a cynical move in an election campaign. It represented a bold effort to open new paths and establish new options for the nation, far ahead of the existing goals of either party.[43] This kind of thinking was exactly what Clifford had earlier prescribed. The president had to be bold and imaginative, and above all had to play the part of a crusader. The Republican Congress had to be held responsible for the lack of constructive legislation that the country needed.

Some scholars believe that Wallace did exert pressure on the president on the civil rights issue. Barton Bernstein, for instance, in a recently published essay, has written: "Wallace's candidacy compelled the President to take a stronger position on civil rights. Only by moving to the left could Truman prevent a bolt of important numbers of urban Negroes and some white liberals from the uneasy Democratic coalition; without their substantial support, he and many urban Democrats were doomed to defeat." [44] William Berman, a student of civil rights in the Truman years, also maintains that the Wallace forces had an impact on the president.[45] To a degree both of these men are correct. However, what is often overlooked is the feared black defection to the Republican party.

On Janurary 8, a memorandum entitled "A Minimum Civil Rights Program for the Eightieth Congress" was written. The document maintained that the Republican leadership should be confronted with the civil rights struggle, and the public should be made to realize that many Republicans were opposed to civil rights legislation. "It's about time the Republicans were forced to take the rap for their own dirty game." [46] On February 2, the president sent his civil rights message to Congress.

Truman was acting on the recommendations of the President's Committee on Civil Rights, which issued its report, *To Secure These Rights,* on October 1947.[47] This substantial report, coupled with pressure from black leaders, as well as cognizance of the political damage that could come from both Wallace and Republican gains with black voters, caused Truman to do something about the condition of the nation's black population. Politically, the fear at the time of the February message was centered more upon the possibility that black voters would return to the party of Lincoln than upon the possibility that they would stray to the party of Wallace. "There are several straws, aside from the loyalty of his leaders to Dewey, that the northern Negro is today ready to swing back to his traditional moorings—the Republican Party," wrote Clifford in his November 1947 memo to the president.[48]

On April 20, William L. Batt, Jr., head of the Democratic party's research division, sent a confidential memorandum to the party's executive secretary, Gael Sullivan, concerning the black vote in New York City. The communication reported that a great number of the city's Negro population were going to vote for Wallace. Batt suggested that this vote could be salvaged and listed some steps that might be taken toward achieving this goal. The key proposal focused on the executive orders promised by Truman in his civil rights message, for the president had said that he would issue orders establishing an FEPC for the government and orders ending discrimination in the armed forces.[49] Batt was certain that these two proposals were most important for regaining the black vote. There is other evidence to show that the Wallaceites were considered to *some degree*. Raymond Pace Alexander, a black lawyer of no small reputation, wrote to Batt, arguing that the nation's black population ought to be made to realize that the Wallace party "is strictly a far left, red tinted, Communistic setup and the only way the present followers can be shaken from Wallace's grip is to expose his fellow travellers in their true light." [50]

However, a little more than a month later, Alexander wrote to Pennsylvania Senator Frank Myers concerning Negro support for the Democratic party. In this letter Alexander spoke of the danger of Republican inroads. Throughout the country the GOP had been trying to garner black votes, and Alexander concluded that "The results, I am very frank to say, have shown that the Republicans have made some real progress and it appears at this writing that in many respects we have permitted them to carry the ball and take the play completely away from us, to our very severe loss." [51] Alexander, however, did not feel that all was lost. After a meeting with Batt, he drew up certain suggestions that he thought would prevent these votes from going to the Republicans. In his six page letter, he never once mentioned the possibility of blacks supporting the Progressive party. He stated that the Democrats had to show the Negroes that they had more to offer them than the Republicans.

The complexities surrounding civil rights do not end here. On August 11, 1948, Batt wrote to Clifford suggesting that civil rights be one of the topics that the president discuss in his campaign trip to California. "The President should discuss Civil Rights in California to cut into Wallace's strength" are the words that Batt used, and these are almost precisely the words that Clifford used in an August 17 memo to the president concerning the 1948 campaign.[52] This evidence indicates that the strategy makers of the Democratic party were paying some attention to the Wallaceites as deep into the election year as August.

Despite the documentation concerning the black vote, there is contrary evidence regarding the importance of the Progressive party's role in the 1948 election as a whole. In July 1966 when Batt was interviewed for the Truman Library, he recalled that the Eightieth Congress had been the major issue of the campaign. Batt remembered "that the Wallaceites wanted to make foreign policy a big issue. We were concerned about the Wallace people and about the Thurmond people but I don't think we sweat much blood over them because obviously you had to fight the Republicans." [53] Queried about the black vote, Batt explained that it had been deemed "quite important." He did not, however, discuss the expected impact of the Wallace candidacy on the Negro vote. During a personal interview on July 2, 1971, Batt said that he had difficulty recalling the Wallace party's role in the Democratic campaign because in his estimation it had been very negligible.[54]

Supportive of Batt's position is the testimony of Kenneth M. Birkhead. Birkhead was recruited by Batt to serve as the anti-Wallace propagandist in the research division of the Democratic party.[55] (In his November 1947 memo, Clifford advised that a Wallace expert be retained.) But Birkhead actually did very little work on the Wallace movement.

There was a time. I was not that close to Mr. Truman or the top side to be able to point specifically to a time, but I don't think there was any question but that there was a decision made some place along the line, that the less said about the Wallace movement the better. Because I had, originally, as I say, been brought to Washington—and it was quite definite, and Batt indicated to me that this was what he had discussed with the people in the White House and the national committee —specifically why I was coming to Washington was to be an advisor and consultant and preparer of materials and whatever it was, in connection with the Wallace movement. It wasn't too long after I came to Washington that the Wallace movement was just dropped, and I don't remember that I was ever told "Forget Wallace, we're not going to mention him," but it was obvious what had happened.[56]

So, Birkhead's evidence reveals that the Democratic party paid little attention to the Wallace "threat" from the time the anti-Wallace expert was added to the research staff. As for the black vote, Birkhead had thought it "vital" and had been afraid that Wallace would capture some of it.[57] Nevertheless, it is clear from Birkhead's interview that after a time, the higher echelons of the Democratic party ceased thinking of Henry Wallace as a major threat. Certainly a keen eye would be kept on the activities of the Progressives, and upon occasion these heretics would be taken into account, but by and large they were to be ignored.

Other facts also point to the conclusion that the Democratic party tended to pay scant attention to Wallace's candidacy. First, the president made only one major civil rights speech from the beginning of his "nonpolitical" trip in June, to election day in November. That one speech was on October 29 and was delivered in Harlem. In August Batt had suggested to Clifford and Clifford had in turn recommended to Mr. Truman that "In New York the President should appear for a major speech at a mass meeting in Harlem, a center of Negro population. His appearance there would have a powerful effect on Negro voters throughout the United States." [58] The party organization's summary of this brief Harlem speech reads as follows: "We must try to attain the goal of equal rights and equal opportunity toward which the things recommended by the Civil Rights Committee lead us." [59] The president's campaign, which put little emphasis on civil rights, tends to bolster the argument that it was not the Progressives who were pushing Truman. At the same time, the Democratic party came out with what people at the time considered a very strong position on civil rights. "We highly commend President Harry S. Truman for his courageous stand on the issue of civil rights.

"We call upon the Congress to support our President in guaranteeing these basic and fundamental American Principles: (1) the right of full and equal political participation; (2) the right to equal opportunity of employment; (3) the right of security of person; (4) and the right of equal treatment in the service and defense of our nation." [60] Irwin Ross reports that the administration did not want a strong civil rights plank and that in the end, even these few words were forced on Truman.[61] In summary, on the crucial issue of civil rights, as well as in general campaign strategy, it was not the Progressive party that served as the major impetus for action. Rather the administration moved in a very cautious manner when prodded by different forces. The main force, however, was the fear of Republicans picking up support on issues and turning that support into votes.

Foreign policy was the issue that had brought the Progressive party into existence, but this was certainly not the *major* concern of the Democrats in 1948. Mr. Truman himself has written that "One of the things I tried to keep out of the campaign was foreign policy." [62] The president did not stress foreign affairs as an issue, nor did he ever suggest that he had any doubts about the wisdom of the nation's foreign policy. Henry Wallace's hopes for a meaningful dialogue with Truman were dashed in 1948 because of increasing tension between the United States and the Soviet Union. While Wallace was crusading for a more reasonable attitude toward Russia, action in Europe did much to undermine his cause. In February Czechoslovakia had come under Communist domination, and in March Czech Foreign Minister Jan Masaryk met his death under strange circumstances.[63] If these events did not cause enough trouble for Wallace, incidents in June and during the summer months caused more damage. On June 23 all travel, other than by air, was halted by the Soviets from the West to Berlin. On June 27 the United

States along with Britain began the famous Berlin airlift, which lasted into the Spring of 1949. Wallace's attempts to make foreign policy a major issue in 1948 could not have survived the events that occurred. The Russians were portrayed as aggressors seeking world domination, and rather than debate foreign policy, the president merely had to show the American people what kind of rascals he was dealing with. There are many implications that can be drawn from this line of reasoning including Richard Freeland's very provocative argument in *The Truman Doctrine and the Origins of McCarthyism*:

> This book argues that the emotional and political forces and the patterns of belief—what in aggregate might be called the "Cold War consensus"—that were to provide the essential energies of postwar anti-Communism were quite fully developed by early 1948. . . . These emotions were aroused and these patterns developed it is argued, as the result of a deliberate and highly organized effort by the Truman administration in 1947–8 to mobilize support for the program of economic assistance to Europe called the European Recovery Program, or Marshall Plan.[64]

The American people had been led to believe that the Soviet Union was their number one enemy, and no matter what Henry Wallace said, the voters were not about to believe him over President Truman.

While Truman did not focus on foreign policy *as such,* he was able to employ the anti-Communist supposition of U.S. foreign actions in his campaign against Wallace. Mention has already been made of the president's March 17, New York City remarks regarding Wallace. He again struck at the former vice-president and his followers on March 29 at a Washington, D.C., dinner of a Greek fraternal order. *Time* Magazine reported the scene this way:

> "The Greeks also had a Henry Wallace," said the President, but he thought the man was Alcibiades (450–404 B.C.), who deserted Athens for its enemy Sparta,

deserted Sparta to return to Athens. "He was the greatest demagogue of all time," said the President. "We
are now facing the same danger to this country. . . .
If imitators of that ancient Greek conqueror want to see
its liberties subverted, he ought to go to the country he
loves so well and help them against his own country." [65]

The *New York Times* reported the story as front page news
saying that the president had "bitterly denounced" Wallace,
which indeed he had.[66] Quite obviously, at the end of
March, Truman was not mellowing in his views toward the
third-party leader. In fact, the president was making it clear
that he had no use at all for the Wallaceites.

In spite of the fact that the Democratic party was not prepared to debate Wallace on his terms, the organization was
cognizant of Wallace's potential impact. William Batt's and
Kenneth Birkhead's testimony notwithstanding, the research
division did do a work-up on Wallace in June. On the
twenty-first, Batt wrote to Democratic National Committee
Chairman J. Howard McGrath and Publicity Director Jack
Redding explaining that his group had collected information
on Wallace. The information was compiled and put together
as a pamphlet "on the belief that the best way to cut the
ground beneath Henry Wallace is to show that Wallace is
not trustworthy, has no consistent policy, and does not have
the capacity to be a successful President." [67] Batt continued,
addressing himself to what the pamphlet was designed to do:
"We felt that lambasting Wallace as a 'Communist' simply
reinforces the martyr feelings of his followers. The pamphlet
reveals very clearly that Wallace is surrounded by pro-Com-
munist advisers, but does not make his Communist tendencies the principal issue. His confusion of mind is his most
vulnerable point with his present following." [68] Batt advised
that various groups become involved in distributing the document, and he finished his memo by asking for "guidance."
The significance of the Wallace pamphlet is difficult to ascertain, but what it seems to indicate is that the Democrats,
while not diverting their full attention to the Wallace candi-

dacy, continued to keep his operations under their scrutiny. This behavior, however, does not contradict the notion that the Democrats at the national level were paying only slight attention to him. The evidence at hand shows that the Progressives were acknowledged throughout the entire election year but that they were not the focal point of campaign strategy.

The interrelationship between foreign policy in general and anti-Communism in the United States provided the framework for the administration's attacks on the third party. Wallace's views on Communism showed his confusion about things generally, argued the Trumanites. How could *his* kind of foreign policy benefit the United States? Of course, it could not. The Democrats' position was unequivocally spelled out in their platform, which fully supported the Truman foreign policy.[69] This support had to be the case since Truman as incumbent had no real difficulty in obtaining the nomination. Clifford had advised that the president's acceptance speech "keynote the entire campaign." [70] With respect to foreign policy, Truman again reiterated his position. The country had "to accept its full responsibility for leadership in international affairs." [71] At the same time, the country had to maintain its commitment to the United Nations. Truman then spoke of bipartisanship in foreign policy; the Progressives had struck at this issue, but apparently to no avail. "As I have said time and time again, foreign policy should be the policy of the whole Nation and not the policy of one party or the other. Partisanship should stop at the water's edge; and I shall continue to preach that through this whole campaign." [72] The speech must have been a great disappointment to the Wallaceites because the president gave no indication of moving toward the goals of the third party. It is quite obvious that Wallace and his supporters had not made the impact on the administration that they had hoped for.[73]

Despite Truman's stance there are still those who argue that the Democrats were pushed by the Progressives in the foreign policy area. Two specific occurrences support this thesis, but at the same time, evidence may be presented to refute it. In the first instance Wallace directed an open letter to Joseph Stalin in early May, which was answered by the Russian premier.[74] From this it could follow that Wallace had opened up an area of communications for Truman and Stalin. However, the fact is that the administration ignored this attempt at better relations between the United States and the USSR.[75] The second and more spectacular action is the now famous abortive Vinson mission. In this episode, which took place in early October, the president assigned Chief Justice Fred Vinson to go to the Soviet Union for talks with Stalin. However, the mission was cancelled before it got under way. Wallaceites have since argued that they were responsible for influencing the president to create this mission, but a closer look at the evidence does not lend much weight to the argument. While Truman has maintained that the Progressives were to some degree in his mind when he developed the Vinson mission,[76] they were not the main catalysts. By October the Progressives were not very much of a threat, and furthermore, Truman had not been moved by them in policy making.

The postconvention Democratic campaign opened on Labor Day, September 6, in Detroit's Cadillac Square. In preparation for this very important speech that would kick off the Fall Democratic effort, George Elsey suggested that the "Republican and the Progressive philosophies" be attacked. Elsey maintained that "The President should attack the Progressive Party by exploding the theory that a splinter group can succeed by pointing out that the real enemy is 'boom and bust' and that the liberals must stick together." [77] Apparently, however, this suggestion was put aside, for a perusal of the Detroit speech reveals no trace of an attack on the Progressives. This fact says something about the diminished importance of the third party in Democratic thinking.

Truman went on to speak of the third party in only four speeches during the Fall campaign. The first occasion was in

Los Angeles on September 23. Speaking at Gilmore stadium he delivered an attack on the Republicans and then shifted gears by saying:

> While I am talking about the forces of progressive liberalism, I want to add a word to all the people of California who believe in liberal ideas.
>
> You, like Americans everywhere today, are disturbed about the threat to peace and the failures of the 80th Congress to deal with basic economic problems here at home.
>
> Most of the people realize that the Democratic administration is doing everything that can be done to preserve the peace. And they realize that the Democratic administration is eager to put an end to the reactionary policies of the 80th Congress.
>
> There are, however, some people with true liberal convictions, whose worry over the state of the world has caused them to lean toward a third party.
>
> To these liberals I would say in all sincerity: Think again.
>
> The fact that the Communists are guiding and using the third party shows that the party does not represent American ideals. . . .
>
> The third party has no power in the government and no chance of achieving power. The simple fact is that the third party cannot achieve peace, because it is powerless. It cannot achieve better conditions here at home, because it is powerless. . . .
>
> A vote for the third party can only weaken the efforts of the Democratic Party to build a healthy nation and a peaceful world.
>
> A vote for the third party plays into the hands of the Republican forces of reaction, whose aims are directly opposed to the aims of American liberalism.
>
> A vote for the third party will not promote the cause of American liberalism; it will injure it.
>
> I say to those disturbed liberals who have been sitting uncertainly on the outskirts of the third party: Think again. Don't waste your vote.[78]

Voting for the Progressive candidate was throwing a vote away, according to the president. Truman explained that the country's foreign policy was predicated on achieving peace and a better way of life. He had said so before and reemphasized this point in Los Angeles. The third party was downright un-American in Truman's view. His stance was as unbending as it had always been toward the new party.

The Los Angeles speech had given rise to a difference of opinion among Truman strategists. The first topic proposed for this talk was "Communism." [79] However, Bill Batt informed Charles Murphy, who along with Clark Clifford headed the president's speechwriting staff, that he was strongly opposed to this kind of talk to a Los Angeles audience. Batt explained that over the years there had been a considerable amount of Communist activity in California, and recently, various levels of California government had passed stringent anti-Communist laws.[80] Secondly, "non-Communist liberals" in the state had been having difficulty trying to clear their organizations of party members.[81] He expressed his overall view on the subject in the following way: "All this means that a speech on Communism by the President would have a very controversial setting. There will be attacks by the Wallaceites. They will attempt to drive liberal Democrats away from the Democratic ticket. There will equally be attacks by the Republicans in an effort to show that their anti-Communist measures have been more effective than those of the federal government." [82] He went on to say that the president should discuss the subject of the speech in advance with prominent California Democrats, especially Helen Douglas and Chet Holifield who were in the midst of the problem in their congressional campaigns.[83] Batt concluded his brief memo by saying, "We feel that the Communist issue should constitute one of the major issues and that it should come early in the campaign, but I doubt that California is the place to make it." [84]

After receiving advice like this, it is conceivable that Truman's aides might have warned him away from attacking the

Progressives. The president, however, was receiving other recommendations as well. In a cable to Truman's appointments secretary, Matthew Connelly, Democratic speech writer Albert Carr reported that a "leading journalist" believed that much could be gained from speaking about the third party in California; however, the journalist did not feel that California was the place for a total attack on the Progressives. The informant had also "pointed out that the support thrown to Chester Bowles and Helen Douglas last night by Henry Wallace opens up other possibilities which should not be ignored." [85] The journalist apparently believed that the Democrats could take advantage of the fact that the Wallace-ites were now selectively supporting some Democrats. Carr reported that he along with Charlie Murphy and speechwriter Dave Bell had faith in the journalist's assessment of the problem.[86] The three then drafted a statement on the third party for insertion toward the end of the speech. With minor changes their draft is what Truman read at Gilmore Stadium.

The speech on communism came in Oklahoma City on September 28. Batt had suggested this locale for the address arguing that "it might be wise to give the speech on the Loyalty Program and our answer to the spy scare here in Oklahoma City. The Middle West, as you know, is where the greatest inroads are being made with this investigation." [87] The author of the first draft of the speech was Stephen J. Spingarn who was on loan to the White House from the treasury department.[88] In a September 16 memo to Clifford, Spingarn had agreed with Batt that Oklahoma City "would be an appropriate place for the speech." [89] Spingarn today claims that the Wallace candidacy had little if anything to do with the development of the speech. Rather, the impulse and need for such a message came from the Alger Hiss case that was causing problems at the time for the Democrats.[90]

In the speech, however, Truman was skillfully able to once again link Communists to the third party. Truman asked why Communists were supporting the third party and answered by saying that they wanted a Republican victory. "The Communists feel that by backing the third party they will take votes away from the Democratic ticket and thus elect a Republican President. . . . The Communists hate the Democratic administration, because of this country's strong foreign policy, and because the economic and social gains which we have put through make it impossible for them to make any progress whatever in this country." [91] The Democrats remained unchanged in their position toward the Soviet Union while telling the voters that the Progressives had been duped by the Communists. As Alan Harper writes:

> What clear effect the Communist issue had in 1948 was to the President's advantage. It accounted for the dramatic evaporation of "Gideon's Army," which, like Byron's Sennacherib, melted like snow. The purification of the Truman candidacy occasioned by Wallace's defection in the first place, and the return of potential Progressives to the Democrats after the new party's Communist support became evident, may have made the difference between victory and defeat.[92]

The Democrats kept the public aware of the Progressive Party's alleged un-American stance through even the final segments of the campaign. Speechwriter John Franklin Carter advised that Truman attack the Wallaceites in a September 30 speech in Louisville, by saying of them, "On the left advances the Communist Republican Party led by Mr. Wallace," a sentence that the president did not employ. Carter revealed that he and Charles Murphy believed that the voters had to be made aware of the fact that a vote for the Wallace cause was actually a vote for Thomas E. Dewey.[93] Others, as well, advised the president to attack the Progressives; among them was former Roosevelt adviser Samuel Rosenman, who expressed his views in a letter dated October 26.[94] Mr. Truman did strike at the Progressives in speeches on October 27 in Boston and October 29 in Brooklyn. In both instances he reminded the electorate that the Commu-

nists were trying to beat him and elect a Republican by supporting a third party.[95]

An ironic fact concerning Truman's attacks on the Wallaceites is revealed in a 1953 interview with the former president. When asked about the attacks, he said that he remembered only his St. Patrick's day reference to Wallace. He then
added that he had accused Wallace of being "friendly to the
Communist program" but that he "never thought that Wallace himself was a Communist." [96] Truman's remarks indicate that the Wallace candidacy had little impact on him,
but they also indicate something far deeper. Harry Truman
did not seem to have any idea that his words about a former
vice-president of the United States probably had the effect
of readying the people of this country for the witch-hunt
that became known as McCarthyism. By hurling charges of
Communism at the third party, the president had fully legitimized the issue for use in American politics.

On the whole the image that Truman tried to present may
be summed up in the words "practical liberalism." His objective was to show that the Democratic party was the party
of the common man standing squarely in the New Deal tradition. The guidelines had been laid down by Clifford in
November 1947, and in August they were reaffirmed by
William Batt and Clifford himself. In his memo to Clifford
of August 11, Batt explained that the research division felt
that there were four principal goals that the president should
aim at in the campaign. The first goal was to win most of
the independent vote "by driving home to the people the
failures of the 80th Congress, and by linking Thomas E.
Dewey closely to the leadership of that Congress." [97] A second goal was to make certain that "the working people, the
veterans, and the Negroes" kept their allegiance to the party.
A third objective was "To cut through all party lines by
showing that the policy of the Truman administration has
kept the nation on a road leading to peace, not to war."
Finally the president was to be shown as a "crusader" who
saved the New Deal and pushed ahead in his own difficult

presidency. Clifford obviously subscribed to these ideas, for they were presented to the president a few days later.[98] By emphasizing these goals, the president would indeed present a liberal image, the kind of image that Truman's advisors and the president himself felt was necessary to win in 1948. He was able to give the rhetorical illusion of shifting to the left without actually making the shift. With respect to civil rights, the black population had gained; but Truman had been pushed into action because of the political exigencies of the time. On foreign policy there was no shift at all, but there did not have to be in order to emerge victorious. In other areas, like the repeal of the Taft-Hartley, there was talk, but it appears to have just been election rhetoric. It is a hard and cold fact that the Wallace forces did not push the Democratic party into new positions. The fabled Truman shift did not occur.

VI

LIBERALS AND 1948

The emergence of a third party based on a more conciliatory foreign policy toward the Soviet Union brought to the forefront of American politics certain questions that had been plaguing liberals for years. The central issue was whether or not non-Communists and Communist party members could work together in liberal organizations in the United States. The emerging cold war created the showdown for liberals, over the Communist issue.[1] No longer could fence sitting be permitted. Men and women were forced to decide whether or not it was possible to embrace liberalism while criticizing U.S. foreign policy. For a man like Norman Thomas, the decision was an obvious one.

> Personally, I should find it as hard to support Mr. Wallace as long as he condones human slavery under Stalin as I would to supporting a well-intentioned man who condoned slavery under Hitler. I am opposed to war with Russia because as a method war would be destructive of its own alleged purposes and of all we care most for, but I do not think that we can successfully avert war by condoning a movement destructive of the things that for you and me make life most worth living. And such a movement, alas, Communism under Stalin has become.[2]

Thomas concentrated most of his fire on the Progressives in 1948 rather than on the Democrats or on the Republicans.[3] However, the Socialist party had very little influence on the American political scene in 1948. It remained for another group to put Wallace under constant attack, and this organi-

zation was the anti-Communist Americans for Democratic
Action.

The year 1948 marked a crucial point in the then brief
history of the ADA. As an organization it was composed of
anti-Communist, New Deal liberals who had come together
in January 1947. Facing its first national political election,
the ADA was playing for high stakes: it was seeking to become the major voice of liberalism in the United States. To
accomplish this goal, the group had to discredit the Wallace
third-party movement. Throughout the campaign the ADA
would engage in various endeavors to demonstrate how un-
American the Wallaceites were, while making certain to
champion their own patriotism.

Following the end of World War II, the liberal community in the United States divided over the issue of cooperation with Communists. During the 1930s and especially
during the war, it had been possible to coexist with the Communist party, but the cold war made that situation intoler-
able to many of the country's liberals. The division among
the liberal ranks emerged most graphically in the correspondence section of the *New Republic*. In the May 13, 1946, issue, James Loeb, Jr., then an officer in the Union for Democratic Action and soon to be an important official in the ADA,
attacked the idea of united front organizations, explaining
that it was impossible to keep them from simply becoming
fronts.[4] The next issue of the *New Republic* had a reply to
Loeb by Stanley Isaacs who was in fundamental disagreement.
Isaacs, who was a New York UDA member, spoke forcefully
saying, "I disagree wholly with his thesis that Communists
must be excluded from organizations supporting a progressive
cause."[5] The issue had been brought to a head, and in the
next several weeks, the *New Republic* served as a forum for
debate over whether or not it was possible for liberals to
work with Communists in the United States.

Michael Straight, the then youthful publisher of the journal, has revealed that he had promised Loeb that his magazine would present an editorial at the conclusion of the

discussion endorsing Loeb's position. The editorial, however, never appeared, for Wallace took over the editorship of the magazine,[6] and his views obviously opposed those of Loeb. What did occur, though, was the development of two different liberal organizations split along the lines of the Loeb-Isaacs arguments. One was the Americans for Democratic Action, and the other was the Progressive Citizens of America, mainly growing out of the National Citizens Political Action Committee and the Independent Citizens Committee for the Arts, Sciences and Professions.[7] The chief difference between the two groups centered on the Communist issue. On January 4, 1947, as part of its founding principles, the ADA issued a statement indicating that its position was unequivocal.

> Within the general framework of present American foreign policy steps must be taken to raise standards of living and support civil and political freedoms everywhere. These policies are in the great democratic tradition of Jefferson, Jackson, Lincoln, Wilson, and Franklin D. Roosevelt. We reject any association with Communists or sympathizers with communism in the United States as completely as we reject any association with fascists or their sympathizers. Both are hostile to the principles of freedom and democracy on which the Republic has grown great.[8]

The noble Eleanor Roosevelt, who had helped to create the new organization, wrote in defense of it: "The American Communists seem to have succeeded very well in jeopardizing whatever the liberals work for. Therefore, to keep them out of policy-making and staff positions seems to be very essential even at the price of being called red-baiters, which I hope no member of this new group will really be." [9] The time was fraught with tension and anxiety over U.S.-Russian relations, and the ADA had chosen to exclude Communists from its ranks. Most members probably believed as Eleanor Roosevelt did that the time had come to drive Communists from the ranks of liberal organizations to prevent their hamstringing those groups. The PCA, however, preferred to follow another line of reasoning and pinned its hopes on the nation's most notable critic of foreign policy, Henry Wallace.

Wallace's resignation from the Cabinet in 1946 had created much liberal disenchantment with the Truman administration. But throughout 1947 as Wallace attacked U.S. foreign policy, the ADA in turn criticized his statements. In April 1947 when Wallace traveled to Europe he continued to be openly critical of America's cold war posture. In England, for instance, he commented on what he thought were the attitudes of many American officials concerning a United States Empire, by discussing a *Life* Magazine article by James Burnham. "It is so wild and mad a nightmare that even many supporters of the present policy must disown it. Yet this position of ruthless imperialism is the position which all groups blinded by hatred of Russia must ultimately defend." [10] Wallace believed that he was speaking for the American Liberal community. In his view the conciliatory policy of the Roosevelt administration toward the Soviet Union had been abandoned and replaced by an intransigent stand forged by the Truman administration. But the ADA disagreed with the former vice-president's statements. Through its newspaper, the *ADA World,* the organization editorially attacked Wallace's statements explaining that "To the extent that Mr. Wallace's journey may have created the mistaken impression that his opinions are the sole voice of liberalism, we will continue to strive to correct that illusion." [11] On June 18 the *World* quoted a telegram from Leon Henderson, chairman of the ADA's Executive Committee in 1947, to Wisconsin Congressman Alvin E. O'Konski, saying that the ADA was in opposition to Wallace's views on foreign policy and further that it did not believe that liberals could cooperate with Communists in this country.[12]

The problem of defining the term liberal was as difficult in the 1940s as it is today. Wallace and his supporters thought themselves the heirs to and the champions of the Liberal movement. The key proposition for this group was an unaggressive foreign policy.

> Liberalism is a recognition that there is no justifiable reason for another war; that there is no condition carrying the seeds of war which can be remedied by force or threat of force. . . .
>
> Here in the United States today, liberalism demands an all-out fight against those who pervert the language of democracy as they advance programs which contravine democracy. It demands opposition to those who breed fear of ideas, and it requires opposition to the criminal political practices of "red-baiting." Liberalism cannot accept traffic in the fear of a word. The word "communist" has become a far greater menace to the American economic and political system than the actual ideology of the Communists. The perversion of this word has made it a weapon for all those who want to blot out reason, eliminate discussion, and cause people to respond from fear. Liberalism—a faith in the collective judgments of the people as it is democratically expressed—cannot condone demagogy.[13]

But just as Wallaceites had their vision of liberalism, so too did the ADA have its view. The ADA's notion of liberalism was expressed and received wide public notoriety in an article written by its 1947 national chairman, Wilson Wyatt, for the *New York Times Magazine*. In a "Creed for Liberals" Wyatt presented ten propositions that he believed demonstrated a liberal philosophy. These were a belief in the judgment of the "ordinary man"; an acceptance of planning; an acceptance of governmental intervention in the field of domestic welfare; a rejection of a "double standard of political morality"; criticism of too much power in too few hands; rejection of "narrow nationalism"; rejection of those people who had dual political allegiances; criticism of the House Un-American Activities Committee; unhesitating support of the Marshall Plan; and a belief that democracy was a common goal throughout the world.[14]

Following his list Wyatt revealed that the principles represented his own feelings, but he indicated that the "essence of
liberalism" was presented in the preamble statement of the
ADA.

> Liberalism is a demanding faith. It rests neither on a set
> of dogmas nor on a blueprint but is rather a spirit which
> each generation of liberals must learn to apply to the
> needs of its own time. The spirit itself is unchanging—
> a deep belief in the dignity of man and an awareness of
> human fraility, a faith in human reason and the power
> of free inquiry, a high sense of individual responsibility
> for one's self and one's neighbor, a conviction that the
> best society is a brotherhood that enables the great num-
> bers of its members to develop their potentialities to the
> utmost.
>
> Opposed to this spirit have always been the wealth
> and power of the organized forces of reaction which to-
> day find their most virulent expression at home and
> abroad in fascism. In our time the democratic idea is
> also threatened by the Communist forces that reject
> democratic values of truth, justice and freedom in the
> interests of a police state.[15]

Wyatt had more to say about the very emotional topic of
Communism and he linked his ideas closely to what, at the
time he was writing, was a possible third-party movement
that might be led by Henry Wallace.

In Wyatt's opinion, which was certainly indicative of the
cold war, Communists could "divide, confuse and paralyze
liberal organizations." [16] Essentially the ADA's national
chairman was offering the same argument that James Loeb
had presented in his 1946 *New Republic* letter. Wyatt was
apparently convinced, as were so many other Americans,
that the Communists were trying to encircle the world and
that in some way his organization could serve in the defense
of the United States against the onslaught. Wyatt was definitely against a third-party movement in the United States.
He felt that such a venture would hurt the liberal cause in

America and help conservatives and Communists. Further, he maintained that the sponsors of such a move were not genuine progressives and were leading Wallace down a disastrous path.[17] In fact, just three days before his article appeared, Wyatt's speech to the American Veterans Committee was quoted by the *ADA World* regarding a possible third party: "However naively and innocently done, it would merely advance the causes of Communism and Fascism and do injury, not to reaction, but to liberal democracy itself" [18] As events progressed, the third party became the focal point of the ADA's criticism during the 1948 campaign.

When Wallace announced his decision to run as a third-party candidate, he obviously anticipated criticism of his position. To counter possible political embarrassment, Wallace, in a sense, issued a declaration of conscience.

> I insist that the United States will not be fully secure until there is real peace between this country and Russia and until there is an international police force stronger than the military establishment of any nation, including Russia and the United States. I am utterly against any kind of imperialism or expansionism whether sponsored by Britain, Russia or the United States, and I call on Russia as well as the United States to look at all our differences objectively and free from the prejudice which the hatemongers have engendered on both sides.[19]

This comment, however, was not nearly enough to satisfy critics of the new party. The Wallaceites had chosen to fight outside of the established two-party system, and for this decision they would pay dearly.

The Americans for Democratic Action, as an organization, believed that Wallace represented a movement that could do serious injury to the goals it was seeking. James Loeb in his capacity as national executive secretary wrote a letter on January 14, 1948, in which he explained, "We believe that, in this first year of work, we have made enormous strides in establishing the bases for a genuine non-Communist liberal movement; but there are tremendous tasks ahead, made particularly difficult by what we consider the irresponsible third party candidacy of Mr. Wallace." [20] In these words one can detect the self-interest that, coupled with fear of the Soviet Union, would impel the ADA to carry on its crusade against Wallace. And, of course, it was Wallace's foreign policy stands and his refusal to drive Communists from the ranks of his supporters which the ADA would persistently attack. On January 22 Loeb wrote that "it is on foreign policy that Wallace is running, and I do not see how any socialist can accept that foreign policy. Every vote for Wallace is a vote against the hopes and the very life of all European socialists." [21] By 1948 the ADA had fused liberalism and anti-Communism. One had to be staunchly anti-Russia to fit into the ADA's liberal niche, and hindsight provides an explanation for this fact. In its attempt to make liberalism respectable and at the same time bestow on itself the leadership of the movement, the organization had to work with a dedicated enthusiasm to discredit the Wallace party. Only in this way could it emerge triumphant in the expected Democratic disaster of 1948.

As could be expected, the ADA was not completely successful in persuading all liberals to accept its position on Wallace. Aside from Wallace himself, the most noteworthy New Dealer to oppose the ADA's stand was former brain trust member Rexford G. Tugwell. Tugwell had been a member of the ADA but had refused an invitation to attend the organization's national convention to be held in February 1948. He declined because he felt that the ADA was disrupting the American liberal community. Tugwell wrote Leon Henderson the following with respect to Wallace:

> Henry Wallace has spoken with increasing strength and clarity straight out of his mind and heart with cold and fearless logic. His actions and his analysis have been those of a man with conscientious concern for the American tradition of progressive action. Your group is inclined to be critical of him for appeasing communists. He has clearly done no such thing; he has merely re-

fused to be confused by a bogey as old as American politics. I have come to believe that this A.D.A. criticism is being used to conceal the frightened consent of the A.D.A. group to an aggressive and dangerous foreign policy and to its reactionary concomitant in domestic life.[22]

After the election, Tugwell, writing in the *Progressive,* reflected on his Progressive party experience. Indicating some remorse about having supported Wallace, he was not sorry for having repudiated the ADA.[23]

The former Roosevelt advisor acknowledged that Communists had been active in the third party, but he had an explanation for the role they played. "The reason Communist workers were so prominent in the Wallace campaign was that the Progressives were—well, where were they? Sitting it out; wringing their hands; and wailing about the wickedness of the Reds." [24] Because so many important New Deal personalities rejected the Wallace movement, a vacuum was created which, according to Tugwell, was filled by members of the Communist party. He also speculated as to what might have been if the forces of progressivism had banded together behind a new party.[25] According to Tugwell's most recent testimony, he knew that Communists were active in the party, and by the summer it was clear that Wallace would not get nearly as many votes as had been anticipated. Consequently, Tugwell did very little campaigning for the Progressive cause but stayed with it in the hope that it would cause a shift in the Democratic party's policies.[26]

In a rejoinder to the Tugwell article, then acting chairman of the ADA, Hubert Humphrey, commented: "On one level the article is a significant confessional; it represents, I believe, the first public admission by a prominent member of the Progressive Party that the Communists dominated the Wallace campaign." [27] Humphrey pointed out how Machiavellian Communists were and defended the ADA's position during the election. This is the same man who had written to Loeb in March 1948:

The subject everyone is talking about: How can we peacefully and effectively get rid of the present incumbent. There is no enthusiasm for Truman out here. Our right wing CIO and AFL boys are holding tough against the Third Party, but they keep asking me "Who are we for?", the tacit assumption being that we certainly can't be for Truman. The tragedy of our movement is that we have everything except a dramatic and appealing symbol on the national level.

What can we do? I understand there is a lot of maneuvering and finagling going on now. If nothing happens soon we must act. Eisenhower, of course, would be a winning candidate. Douglas might not win. But at the margin we should take Douglas because we not only face defeat in November—we face a possible disintegration of the whole social-democratic block in this country. If we are going to lose, we ought to lose with a good candidate who can help us hold our forces together and, particularly, help us on the Congressional level.[28]

Truly, it would seem that Humphrey was the Machiavellian character in the drama being played out, for he was soon to become the Democratic senatorial candidate from Minnesota, and a strong national ticket would greatly aid him. On April 27th Humphrey informed Loeb of his decision to run but he reminded his friend that "Really there is a chance to win in this election. The only thing that could mess it up would be a strong Third Party candidate." [29] Humphrey, however, was determined to see that possibility negated. His secretary, on March 24, had written to James Wechsler of the *New York Post* requesting material that could be used in an attempt to "smear" Wallace.[30] Minneapolis's mayor was so set on gaining a Senate seat that he was willing to try to dump Truman as well as to bait Wallace.

Another prominent member of the ADA who took up the issue of Communist influence in the Progressive party after the election is Arthur Schlesinger, Jr. In *The Vital Center,* a book that merits the epithet, "bible of postwar liberals," Schlesinger argued that Communists were responsible for the formation of the third party. In his words, "The Wallace movement represented the most considerable undertaking ever attempted by the Communists in the United States." [31] Schlesinger in his distinguished role as author and social critic was instrumental in spreading that view to liberals throughout America.

To be sure, members of the ADA believed the Schlesinger line of argument in 1948, but there was also much to be gained by slamming away at the Communist issue. The ADA made a conscious decision to work against Wallace in the election year. In retrospect, it appears that members of the ADA definitely saw the Wallace movement as a threat to their power. James Loeb wrote in a March 16, 1948, memorandum that the organization had to "take the offensive against Henry Wallace and the third party. Almost every day Wallace is making statements that are a disgrace to the liberal tradition and should be answered." [32] Loeb's accusation is sanctimonious at the very least and again represents a line of thought within the organization, for the ADA had set itself up as the guardian of the liberal tradition in postwar America.

By its use of anti-Communism as a political issue, the ADA was becoming increasingly obvious on the political scene. There are, however, different explanations for the ADA's actions. Johannes Hoeber, former assistant director of the Democratic party's research division in 1948 as well as a past member of the ADA's National Board for that year, believes that the Democratic party and the ADA had an agreement concerning the treatment of Wallace.

> But there was an agreement very early in the campaign, . . . that *the* job that ADA would take on, would be the fight against Henry Wallace. And ADA published a very extensive book on the role of Henry Wallace, as a campaign document. And by mutual agreement, the Research Division stayed out of that area entirely; this was the specialty that the ADA took on. In hindsight I think it was a very wise tactical decision to let

what you might call the left wing of the liberal movement supporting Truman take on the fight against
Wallace rather than the official organization.[33]

While Hoeber's opinion seems plausible, there is no supporting evidence for it. In fact, there is evidence to the
contrary. On the ADA side of the ledger, both James Loeb
and Joseph Rauh have denied that there was an agreement
between the Democrats and the ADA.[34]

On the Democratic side, despite Hoeber's remarks, others
are in disagreement. William Batt, the former director of the
research division and also a former ADA member has denied
the existence of such an arrangement.[35] But more important
are the recollections of Clark Clifford who shows a marked
disdain for the way the organization acted with respect to
trying to select a candidate other than Harry Truman in
1948.[36] Clifford maintains that, in effect, men like Batt were
picked for their positions despite the fact that they were ADA
members—not because of it. Finally, as one looks over the
actions of the Democratic party in 1948, the fact is that the
research division did initially hire Kenneth Birkhead to work
on anti-Wallace propaganda, although as it turned out, he
actually did very little work in that area. However, while no
formal agreement may have existed, one cannot help but
note the overlapping membership of the ADA and the
Democratic party's research division.[37]

Since no official connection between the Democrats and
the ADA can be established with respect to Wallace, the
focus for explaining the ADA's actions must center on its sin-
cere belief that the third party was a Communist-run enter-
prise, and on the practical value of such a belief. When Loeb
suggested that the ADA launch an attack on the Wallace
forces, a pamphlet was proposed. On April 28 the ADA sent
out a letter bearing the signature of its national chairman,
Leon Henderson, explaining that it had published a pamphlet dealing with the Wallace party because of the "great
demand" or information that could be used to support

charges against Wallace and the new party. Henderson added that the analysis was not intended for wide distribution but rather was drawn up for "key leaders and candidates." A charge of one dollar was assessed for the document as well as for the supplementary study that was to follow.[38]

The pamphlet was entitled, *Henry A. Wallace: the First Three Months,* and began by explaining that the ADA had always opposed Wallace's new party and had constantly attempted to challenge Wallace for his "irresponsible" statements.[39] But the task of keeping up with all the former vice-president's statements and evasions, or explanations of his statements, was very difficult. The ADA also insisted that Communists and "apologists" for the Communist party were spearheading the third party movement.[40] The analysis attempted to give "some outstanding examples of the shifts and fallacies appearing in Wallace's campaign record . . . against the background of the formation of the Third Party." [41] The first chapter asserted that the origins of the new party lay in the American Communist party. As proof of this assertion, the ADA quoted various Communist party officials who had sanctioned a third party, as well as a former Wallace supporter. "Dr. Frank Kingdon, Co-chairman of PCA among others, resigned from PCA. Kingdon explained it this way in his New York POST column: 'Who asked Henry Wallace to run? The answer is in the record. The Communist Party, through William Z. Foster and Eugene Dennis, were the first. . . . I was finally convinced when the steamroller ran over me the night PCA became the second organized group to demand the Wallace candidacy.' " [42]

In the second chapter the ADA criticized Wallace for his stand regarding the Communist coup in Czechoslavakia. "In Minneapolis, February 29, 1948, Wallace blamed the Czech coup on the Truman Doctrine and indicated that Russia was retaliating against U.S. aggression." [43] Wallace's running mate was also cited as holding the same position. The next chapter chided Wallace for anti-British and anti-United States sentiments concerning imperialism. The famous 1946

Madison Square Garden speech that precipitated Wallace's break with Truman was quoted, emphasizing his remarks accusing Britain of having an imperialistic foreign policy. In addition, some of his remarks made in England in 1947 were cited. "As one patriotic American I am utterly opposed to this policy of imperialism. I have said in America, and I say again here, that it will end by uniting the world against America and dividing America against itself.

"It is a dangerous programme for America to embark on imperialism. . . . It may cost little to divide the world. But to keep the world divided is beyond the resources of any nation." [44]

The attack continued with a section entitled, "Wallace: Commander-in-Chief," which drew upon some of Wallace's remarks regarding the possibility of war. This part of the study was designed to show that the former vice-president could never be an effective head of state. After quoting from a Wallace remark about the unlikelihood of a war-oriented cabinet in his administration, the ADA stated, "This could only mean that Wallace would have a Secretary of State and Secretary of Defense as ignorant of Communist policy as he claims to be." [45] The account then presented a chapter composed of statements by members of the Roosevelt family demonstrating their opposition to the third party. This chapter was intended to illustrate that Wallace's views did not represent a continuation of New Deal thinking.[46]

Moving on to "Political Blackmail," the ADA attempted to show that the third party was a threat to genuine progressives: "Within three months after Wallace announced for the presidency, the Third Party had established itself as the chief threat to the election of progressives. The Third Party will be used either to: Blackmail progressives into supporting Soviet foreign policy as defined by Wallace supporters," or to "Punish at the polls those progressive candidates who do not come to terms with Wallace forces." [47] To prove the point, the ADA provided examples of progressive Democrats whom the third party opposed at the time.

The analysis also continued to attack Wallace's foreign policy views. For instance, it was critical of comments that he made about United States foreign policy with regard to Italy. Wallace, according to the ADA, had accused America of fermenting civil war in Italy.[48] The presentation concluded on the issue of Communist influence by examining some of the sources of funds for the third party and reporting that "One of the top contributors of $5,000 came from a known Communist, Frederick V. Field, once a contributing editor to the NEW MASSES and a principal contributor to that magazine before it folded." [49]

In the area of domestic policy, specifically civil rights, the ADA maintained that Wallace had a spotty record. The NAACP's *Crisis* was used as a source to show that Wallace as secretary of commerce had done little for the black population. The ADA itself pointed out that "During his regime as Commerce Secretary Wallace insisted that the segregation policy in the National airport restaurant, which was under his jurisdiction, could not be changed." [50] Labor was another area in which the account was critical of Wallace. The organization argued that Wallace had an "unearned reputation as a 'friend of labor.' " [51]

Members of the organization were quite pleased with the pamphlet. On May 3, Wilson Wyatt wrote that "The ADA analysis of the first three months of Wallace's campaign is one of the best publications of its kind I have ever seen done." [52] Professor Schlesinger in his *Vital Center,* which is often looked to as a key work for understanding postwar liberal thinking in America, has included an end note that calls the analysis and its supplement "Indispensible documents for the study of the campaign." [53] Taken with his earlier mentioned statement that Communists were responsible for the formation of the third party, one is forced to conclude that he approved of the ADA analysis.[54] The ADA did not believe that it was damaging the liberal movement by using the Communist issue as its major weapon against the Wallace forces.

The Wallaceites by and large tended to ignore the ADA attacks. According to Curtis MacDougall's chronicle of the Wallace movement, "To offset the ADA attack, the Progressive Party relied upon its general approach. It had no special division to consider the problem of attracting the liberal vote." [55] An examination of the record tends to support MacDougall's contention. The entire Progressive campaign challenged the assumptions of the ADA on anti-Communism. Wallace did criticize the Soviet Union, but that criticism was lost in all of the hysterical shouting of the day. Perhaps the following excerpt from a letter written by Wallace in April 1948 can serve as an example of his attitude.

> With regard to disavowing Communist objectives and methods, I have no hesitancy in saying that I personally believe in progressive capitalism, that I do not believe in the materialistic dialectic, that I do believe in God, that I do not believe that force ever settles anything ultimately. But I utterly refuse to engage in the only kind of red-baiting and Russia denunciation which would momentarily satisfy a Douglas. These people live by hate of Communism and Russia to an extent which governs their whole lives. I utterly and completely refuse to be infected by their fears and hates.[56]

However, there was once a time in the campaign when the former vice-president seemingly yielded to ADA criticism. In June, speaking in Center Sandwich, New Hampshire, Wallace claimed that if the Communists ran a ticket of their own, he would gain three million votes. In 1952 he mused that "my mistake was in not repeating this again and again." [57] Generally though, the Progressives could only hope that the enemy's arguments would not be persuasive enough to draw away large numbers of potential voters.

But the Communist issue was a strong one. James Loeb made an appearance before the platform committee of the Progressive party in July at which he blasted the third party for its un-American behavior.[58] Following his appearance,

Loeb put some of his thoughts about the Progressives in a personal letter.

> I was, as you may have seen, the only unfriendly witness who appeared before the Wallace platform committee. It was quite an experience, I assure you. I do not say that Mr. Wallace is a Communist. Indeed, I know he is not. But I do say, . . . that his party is so completely controlled by the Communists that their withdrawal would mean the complete collapse of the Wallace movement. This judgment is not a fantastic charge. It is based on long experience in the liberal movement and on the knowledge of the personalities involved. I am certain that there are men and women of good will in the Wallace movement, but they are isolated, unorganized, and ineffective. The central political fact of the postwar world is one that Mr. Wallace and his friends insist on overlooking, namely the fact that thousands of men and women who went to concentration camps and in exile fighting fascism are now once more in concentration camps and in exile. In my humble opinion, a vote for Wallace means a vote for totalitarian oppression and dictatorship.[59]

What was lacking from this earnest discussion of the Wallace movement was any mention of what the ADA stood to gain from a smashing defeat of the Progressive forces. Apparently, the ADA was having success in spreading its message, for on August 5, labor leader A. F. Whitney wired Leon Henderson in response to a letter concerning political endorsements, saying that "The Wallace party is in the hands of Communists. Every vote for that party means support for the fascist Republicans." [60] Whitney very obviously was in agreement with the ADA concerning the role of Communists in the new party; and as the 1948 campaign progressed, it became apparent that for most liberal voters, there was little alternative to Harry Truman.

But were the ADA charges accurate is the question that

must concern students of this election. To be sure, according
to Rexford Tugwell and Wallace himself, members of the
Communist party did become active in the Progressive ranks.
However, this author is convinced that Henry Wallace's actions in leading a new party and addressing himself and the
party to foreign policy considerations were consistent with
his own postwar beliefs. By every indication, Wallace sin-
cerely felt that the Truman administration was heightening
the tensions of the cold war. The former vice-president did
not have to be pushed into his 1948 position, for he arrived
at it through his own evolution. Communists were present in
the Progressive party, but they did not control Wallace. As
the 1972 Democratic presidential hopeful, South Dakota Senator George McGovern said, "I wasn't happy with the direction the Democratic Party was taking in those times. I liked
what Wallace had to say about foreign policy. I still think he
was essentially right." [61] However, most Americans did not
and do not today share McGovern's point of view. Rather,
the more widely held perspective was that of the ADA and
the Democratic party.

On September 3, 1948, Joseph Rauh, chairman of the
ADA's Executive Committee, suggested some methods for
achieving more publicity for the organization. Among the
proposals was a call for *"A liberal manifesto against Wallace."* [62] Rauh desired a "very tough statement," and Loeb
outlined what was required to Reinhold Niebuhr, a founding member of ADA and a member of the National Board:
"Our feeling is that we can demonstrate the isolation of Wallace among top-flight liberal and labor leaders by having
them sign a simple statement of conviction with regard to
the third party movement. This statement, we feel, should be
an eloquent appeal to the liberals of America in the name of
American progressive tradition, and specifically of the Roosevelt tradition." [63] What emerged was "An Appeal to the Liberals of America" issued in late October. Harold Ickes's name
appeared on the letter sent out to solicit signatures for the
"Appeal." In response to the Ickes letter, Dean Acheson,

A. A. Berle, Abe Fortas, and many other distinguished liberals, agreed to sign.

The "Appeal," issued on October 23, struck at the contention that there was a connection between Wallace's party and FDR.

> But the name of the party, the candidacy of Henry Wallace and the pretensions to liberalism must not obscure the stark fact that this new movement, in its origin and its objectives, runs counter to the human impulses of American progressivism and to the spirit of Franklin D. Roosevelt. . . .
>
> The Progressive Party breaks sharply with the American democratic tradition. It represents a corruption of American liberalism. It represents, in particular, a repudiation of the methods and purposes of Franklin D. Roosevelt. . . .
>
> In its foreign policy the Progressive Party invites a betrayal of free people throughout the world. . . .
>
> The striking and fundamental divergence between the Progressive Party and Roosevelt's political philosophy is its theory of collaboration with Communists. The Philadelphia convention of the Progressive Party demonstrated conclusively that collaboration with Communists means control by them.

The "Appeal" concluded by endorsing Truman and Alben Barkley.

> The Wallace candidacy represents a fundamental challenge to the liberals of America—to their sense of political responsibility.
>
> We urge all followers of Franklin D. Roosevelt to oppose Henry Wallace and his Progressive Party.
>
> We urge all followers of Franklin D. Roosevelt to vote on November 2nd for Harry S. Truman and Alben W. Barkley.[64]

The endorsement of Truman was a tactical measure to attract signatures, for as Loeb wrote, "The endorsement of Truman should be definitely secondary, but we feel it is necessary because a number of New Dealers would not want to sign a purely negative statement." [65] Henry Wallace had attempted to tie his campaign to the Roosevelt legend. In response, the ADA attempted to stress its claim that Wallace was in fact not the heir to Roosevelt's mantle. The Communist issue, however, was again central to the liberal attack.

The ADA concluded its 1948 campaign against the third party with a supplement to its earlier analysis entitled, *Henry A. Wallace: The Last Seven Months of His Presidential Campaign*. In a two-page conclusion, the organization spelled out its findings. Wallace never should have ventured into a third party because he knew that he would not have any real liberal support.[66] Further, the ADA adopted Truman as its hero on the domestic scene, at least publically: "President Truman—especially in the last six months of the campaign—had proven an intrepid defender of the common man and waged a valiant fight against a hostile and reactionary congress." [67] Concerning foreign policy, the ADA maintained that Wallace would have been more effective if he had rejected Communist support. His defense of Russian actions was criticized and presented as a reason for liberals to shun the new party.[68] The analysis correctly explained that the Wallace movement gave little indication of being able to force a "political realignment" in the country.

Of what significance was the ADA in the Truman victory? Did its slashing attacks on Wallace really keep the undecided from joining the ranks of the Progressive party? Clifton Brock, in his very laudatory account of the ADA, maintains that the body helped serve as a bulwark against Communist attempts to cause a reversal in American foreign policy.[69] Curtis MacDougall, in his very biased account of the Progressive party, very expectedly disagrees with Brock. MacDougall is very critical of the ADA's 1948 tactics because he believes that the organization engaged in red-baiting that was effective with liberals.[70]

The ADA did indeed use the Communist issue unmercifully against Henry Wallace in 1948. The analyses it issued

were filled with charges accusing Wallace of following a Soviet line. The ADA had apparently chosen to attack Wallace
for two different but interrelated reasons. The organization
believed what it was saying and writing about the Progressives concerning Communism, but probably went to such
great length in publicizing its views because it wanted the
leadership of the liberal community. But the country's mood
was changing, and witch-hunts were beginning, and the ADA
was helping, although unwittingly. As Robert Griffith explains in his perceptive treatment of Joseph McCarthy and
the Senate, "Even Democratic liberals such as Hubert H.
Humphrey took to baiting third party candidate Henry Wallace and his followers in an effort to strengthen their own
position as sober, industrious, and 100 percent American re-
formers." [71] Professor Athan Theoharis has also drawn a connection between the ADA's role in the 1948 election and the
McCarthy hysteria of the 1950s.[72] The connection is real.
The ADA, by focusing on Communism and equating anti-
Communism with liberalism, in a time of growing cold war
tension and fear, showed how effectively the issue could be
used in postwar politics. By playing to a fear psychology, the
ADA ironically placed the liberal community in the position
of demonstrating to the right, how anti-Communism could
be effectively used at the national level. At the same time, it
is impossible to calculate how many votes the organization
influenced. What can be concluded, however, is that the ADA
probably convinced many borderline Democratic liberals
that the Progressive party was a Communist-dominated operation. More than any other group, the ADA attacked the
third party; and more than any other group, it benefited
when the third party failed so dismally and left it as the
major liberal organization in the United States.

VII

END RESULTS

On the first Tuesday in November 1948, American voters went to the polls and elected Harry Truman to the presidency. The victory came as a surprise to many people, expert and layman alike, but Mr. Truman had expected it. Privately and publicly, he had predicted his election and this period was his time for gloating.[1]

Truman amassed a popular vote of 24,179,345 while collecting 303 electoral votes. The Progressives, on the other hand, were decimated at the polls, gathering only 1,157,326 votes, which was less than 2.5 percent of the popular vote.[2] Further, in the Electoral College, the Wallace forces did not receive one vote. The Progressives had hoped to show, through a large vote for their party, that they were representative of a line of American thinking that the president had been ignoring in his dealings with the Soviet Union. Instead, the Progressive party, by its dismal showing, indicated that most voters favored the "bipartisan" approach to foreign policy which was ostensibly being followed. On the whole, however, the election had engendered very little enthusiasm among the electorate. One would think that the race between Truman and Dewey, with two other parties, the Dixiecrats and the Progressives, would bring the voters out in droves. Actually, the voter turnout was quite low, proportionally the lowest turnout since 1928. This fact has led political scientists Angus Cambell, Philip Converse, Warren Miller, and Donald Stokes to conclude that "no overriding issues intrude to deflect the electorate from voting with its standing partisan allegiances."[3] The president, aided by his advisors, had picked the right issues at which to punch away.

In retrospect, ironically, Henry Wallace helped Harry Truman achieve victory. Samuel Lubell, in the *Future of American Politics*, shows that the Wallaceites aided Truman substantially in obtaining votes.[4] According to Lubell, "if one traces through the third party bolts which have occurred thus far in the era of Democratic supremacy, . . . the disaffection of one element strengthens the attachment of other elements in the coalition." [5] While the contention seems to lack credence for our recent presidential elections, it was true for 1948. Lubell has demonstrated that Truman's strong anti-Communist position greatly benefited the Democrats in Catholic precincts. Thus, where Truman was hurt by a defection of the left, he was compensated by a gain from conservative types.

> Throughout the country Truman received a record Catholic vote, exceeding in some areas, even Al Smith's showing: The heavy Catholic turnout—perhaps the most astonishing single aspect of Truman's surprising victory—resulted largely from the return to the Democratic party of supporters of Father Coughlin.
>
> That may startle some people who saw Truman's 1948 victory as a triumph of liberalism and as a new swing to the old native left. However, throughout the country one finds a remarkable parallel between Truman's gains and the vote given in Coughlin's Union party in 1936.[6]

On November 5, Wallace wrote to Truman wishing him well.[7] The defeated candidate asked Truman to "promptly end the cold war" explaining that the president could not give the American people what they expected if the cold war persisted.[8] Wallace then added, "You are aware that my supreme concern in the recent campaign was peace. I believed that you had fallen victim to the 'gluttons of special privilege' whose domestic policies you denounced, but whose foreign policies you accepted." [9] Wallace's words accurately indicated his belief that Truman had not moved toward the Progressive party's views on foreign policy. This correspondence contradicts postelection statements, made by the Progressives, claiming credit for making peace a major campaign issue. The Wallaceites had been ineffective in trying to achieve a change of direction in United States foreign policy. The Progressives, having called for a less aggressive foreign policy toward Russia and having received the endorsement of the Communist party, became very vulnerable to attacks from the Democrats, the Americans for Democratic Action, and any other person or persons who chose to exploit the issue of Communism. Red-baiting became quite an effective tactic in the operation aimed at destroying the third party. The stigma of being "soft on Communism" was taken off the Democrats and placed squarely on the Progressives.

Rexford Tugwell wrote to presidential secretary Charles Ross on November 15 suggesting that the president could bring about "national unity" by convincing all of the American people of his desire for peace.[10] Tugwell recommended that the administration send a delegation to Moscow headed by Chief Justice Fred Vinson and including Henry Wallace. He believed that the inclusion of Wallace would put the Russians on the spot and convince the nation that the president really wanted peace.[11] It is difficult to believe that a man as astute as Tugwell was naive enough to think that his plan would be taken seriously. The Democrats, aided by a host of anti-Communist liberals, had just waged a hard-fought campaign where Wallace had been labeled a Communist sympathizer. The tactic had proved an overwhelming success, and it is doubtful, to say the least, that the president would have been receptive to an idea that placed Wallace in the limelight. The Democrats had completely rejected the ideas of the third party, and Truman was not about to reconsider them. Tugwell, however, evidently thought that the Progressives had mustered enough strength to have a positive impact on the president.[12]

It is not surprising to find that writers have already argued that the Wallace candidacy aided Truman in his victory.[13] The important added fact about the Progressive party is that it did not precipitate any shift in domestic or foreign policy. The events of 1948 do not support the conventional wisdom concerning third parties. In fact, a reverse hypothesis is true. The Progressives were set upon for being pro-Russian, and in a time of rampant cold war thinking, their ideas were completely rejected. At the same time, the presence of the third party made it easier for the Democrats to take a hard line on Communism while concentrating their main fire on the Republicans. Former Progressives find it difficult to agree entirely with the foregoing analysis. They believe that the Democrats coopted the Progressive domestic program,[14] but the overall picture does not bear out this belief. From the available evidence, it is clear that Truman's "liberal" campaign was planned in advance of the Wallace candidacy, and more important, it was planned with the Republicans in mind. Truman was supposed to present a liberal image to the voters—no new programs were planned to give substance to this image.

After the election, the *New York Star,* formerly *PM,* editorialized that the Truman victory was also "a victory for most of what Mr. Wallace stands for." [15] The *Star* had endorsed Truman because it felt that the Democratic Party "offered the best vehicle for liberals of all shades." [16] The *New York Times,* however, believed that the third party was a failure. In an editorial entitled, "Mr. Wallace's Tragedy," it wrote: "Third parties have often played a useful part in the past. Many times their programs have been taken over by the major parties and enacted into law. But the abysmal failure of Henry A. Wallace in Tuesday's election proves once and for all time that this country has no room for a third party allied with those whose roots are in foreign soil." [17] By so writing, the *Times* demonstrated that it was convinced that the charges leveled against the Wallaceites were true. *Time* was more temperate and objective when it commented that Truman "did not swing violently to the left. Henry Wallace had tried to lead him that way and he had brushed Wallace off with indifference, even with contempt." [18] *Time* concluded, in effect, that the Progressives exercised no effective leftward pull on the Democratic party.

And what of Henry Wallace's reaction to the debacle of 1948? The former vice-president subscribed to the theory that his party had been an important factor in the election. On November 3, the day following the election, his statement contained the following: "The Progressive Party has pointed out that which time will vindicate—namely, that there can be no solution to these domestic issues until militarism and the 'get tough' foreign policy are repudiated." [19] On the 9th of November, he assured Anita Blaine that "Undoubtedly, the fact that President Truman adopted at least our domestic program is largely responsible for his election." [20] The next day, he was writing that the impact of the party should not be gauged by the amount of votes it collected.[21] But soon Wallace began to drift from this position and from the party itself.

The Korean War precipitated his break with the party. On July 15, 1950, he issued a statement supporting the actions of the Truman administration, and on August 8 he resigned from the Progressive party.[22] On the same day, Wallace wrote to Senator Claude Pepper responding to Pepper's letter of July 26. Pepper had informed Wallace he had met with the president and that Truman had been quite happy with Wallace's decision to support the Korean decision. Pepper also added that Truman had said "that you were the best Secretary of Agriculture we ever had and that, while he had gotten a little mad with you on occasions, he always liked you." [23] The Florida senator also suggested that Wallace might visit the president when he was in Washington. Wallace replied by saying,

> With regard to your luncheon conversation it occurs to me that you might perhaps want to phone or see Pres. Truman and tell him that in case developments are such that he thinks a talk with me might serve the cause of peace, I would be happy to call on him off the record. If President Truman had followed his own heart as I knew it in 1946 we would be on the road to peace today instead of war.[24]

By 1950 then, Wallace had accepted, if grudgingly, the need to back American foreign policy. Of Wallace's change, none other than Hubert Humphrey wrote, "We have been following your activities in recent months with great interest, and I am personally very pleased with your change of views." [25]

The former vice-president also began to alter his position concerning the party that he specifically had led. His essential reason for running never changed through the years. "My purpose in running for President in 1948 was to underline to the American people the importance of a peaceful understanding with Russia," he told a correspondent in 1957,[26] but he neglected to talk about the various changes in foreign policy that he had wanted to see occur. In other words, in the 1950s, Wallace softened his rhetoric about American foreign policy in the years of the cold war. His views did shift more emphatically in his discussion of Communists in the Progressive party. He wrote to Curtis MacDougall, "As I told you before, insofar as I played a part in founding the Progressive Party I acted in the faith and hope that it would be free from domination by any clique including the Communists. I am now convinced that the Communists had a strong influence in the party, especially after the 1948 election." [27] Here was a man, then, who had seen his dream destroyed by the Communists. Wallace's comments on his disillusionment over the party fit well into the stereotyped image that the Democrats and ADA had tried to project. One could argue that Wallace spent the last part of his life trying to justify and apologize, at one and the same time, for his actions in 1948.

And what can be said of the Democrats and their response to the Wallaceites? John E. Barriere, a member of the research division in 1948, believes that the Democrats were not moved by the Progressives in policy matters. In a 1966 interview he recalled:

> About Wallace I think the general idea was that the more liberal and the more aggressive the President was at hammering at the bread and butter issues, the more he would be likely to undercut Wallace's support. I

don't think there was any discussion in the Research Division, and I am sure there was none in my presence, about attempting to suggest that the President should trim his sails on foreign policy to get the left back in.[28]

Barriere's testimony in light of the other evidence presented, is an accurate appraisal of Democratic party strategy. The Wallaceites became the scapegoats of the campaign and, therefore, helped insure Truman's victory. Although ex-Progressives are proud of taking credit for causing a shift in Truman's policies, and, therefore, feeling that they achieved a victory of sorts in 1948, the evidence suggests the opposite. The Progressives inadvertantly helped set up a Democratic victory.

Harry Truman's election in 1948 was not a victory for liberalism. The Democrats as well as the Americans for Democratic Action had red-baited the Progressive party and had sought to perpetuate the United States' hard-line position toward the Sovet Union. On the domestic scene Truman had blasted the "reactionary" Eightieth Congress but seemed to have no desire to achieve his campaign program. Truman, the politician, with the shrewd help of Clark Clifford and other astute advisors as well as anti-Communist liberals, had won what appeared to be a liberal victory. In reality, the electorate voted for an incumbent who promised to keep existing foreign policy intact and to carry on the domestic policies of Franklin Roosevelt. Further, by their own tactics, the "respectable" liberal community led by the president had legitimized red-baiting during a time of growing antagonism between the United States and Russia. The Wallace candidacy, then, not only failed to achieve what it set out to achieve in 1948, it encouraged the Democratic party and its standard-bearer to maintain its old position and power unimpared, while giving the country a real taste of what was to come in later years over the issue of anti-Communism.

NOTES

PREFACE

1. John D. Hicks, *The Populist Revolt* (Minneapolis: University of Minnesota Press, 1931).
2. William B. Hesseltine, *The Rise and Fall of Third Parties* (Washington, D.C.: Public Affairs Press, 1948), pp. 9–10.
3. "The Choice For President," *The Progressive* 12 (September 1948):3.
4. Hesseltine, "The Perversion of Progressivism," in *The Rise and Fall of the Third Parties*, p. 5.
5. Wallace and Baldwin to Los Angeles County Office, Independent Progressive Party, November 4, 1948, Progressive Party Papers, University of Iowa Library.
6. Henry A. Wallace speech to the National Committee of the Progressive Party, November 13, 1948, Henry A. Wallace Papers, University of Iowa Library (hereafter cited as Wallace Papers).
7. Wallace to Curtis MacDougall, December 11, 1952, Progressive Party Papers, University of Iowa Library.
8. Interviews with C. B. Baldwin, September 18, 1971, and Len DeCaux, July 21, 1971.
9. Karl M. Schmidt, *Henry A. Wallace: Quixotic Crusade, 1948* (Syracuse: Syracuse University Press, 1960), p. 91.
10. Harry S. Truman, *Memoirs, II* (New York: Doubleday, 1956), p. 243.
11. Interview by Mrs. Norman Sun for Curtis MacDougall, with Harry S. Truman, May 26, 1953, Progressive Party Papers, University of Iowa Library.
12. Rexford Guy Tugwell, "Progressives and the Presidency," *The Progressive* 13 (April 1949): 5, and interview with Rexford Tugwell, July 22, 1971.
13. David A. Shannon, *The Decline of American Communism* (New York: Harcourt, Brace & Co., 1959), p. 179.
14. Jules Abels, *Out of the Jaws of Victory* (New York: Henry Holt & Co., 1959), p. 4
15. Schmidt, *Henry A. Wallace: Quixotic Crusade* and Curtis D. MacDougall, *Gideon's Army*, 3 vols. (New York: Marzani & Munsell, 1965).
16. Walter LaFeber, *America, Russia, and the Cold War, 1945–1971* (New York: John Wiley, 1967, 1972), p. 73.
17. Richard S. Kirkendall, "Election of 1948," in *History of American Presidential Elections, IV,* ed. Arthur M. Schlesinger (New York:

Chelsea House, 1971), pp. 3099–3145. As recently as January 1972, in a very fine article, Frank Ross Peterson has written "The Progressives are also given credit for forcing the Democratic Party to adopt a more liberal platform then it might have otherwise in order to appeal to its traditional supporters." "Protest Songs for Peace and Freedom: People's Songs and the 1948 Progressives," *Rocky Mountain Social Science Journal* 9 (January 1972): 7. Peterson, however, does not seem to be in full agreement with this thesis since he lists his own reasons for Truman's victory.

CHAPTER I: FOREIGN POLICY SPLITS TWO DEMOCRATS

1. Harry S. Truman, *Memoirs, I* (New York: Doubleday, 1955), p. 19.
2. The following studies discuss Henry Wallace. Frank Kingdon, *An Uncommon Man: Henry Wallace and 60 Million Jobs* (New York: Readers Press, 1945); Russell Lord, *The Wallaces of Iowa* (Boston: Houghton Mifflin, 1947); Edward L. Schapsmeier and Frederick H. Schapsmeier, *Henry A. Wallace of Iowa: The Agrarian Years, 1910–1940* (Ames: Iowa State University Press, 1968), and by the same authors *Prophet in Politics: Henry A. Wallace and the War Years* (Ames: Iowa State University Press, 1970); Curtis D. MacDougall, *Gideon's Army* 3 vols. (New York: Marzani & Munsell, 1965); Karl Schmidt, *Henry A. Wallace: Quixotic Crusade, 1948* (Syracuse: Syracuse Univerity Press, 1960); Dwight MacDonald, *Henry Wallace: The Man and the Myth* (New York: Vanguard Press, 1948); Alonzo L. Hamby, "Harry S. Truman and American Liberalism, 1945–1948" (Ph.D. thesis, University of Missouri, 1965); Norman Markowitz, "The Rise and Fall of the People's Century: Henry Agard Wallace and American Liberalism, 1941–1948" (Ph.D. thesis, University of Michigan, 1970), as well as his 1973 book with the same title; Marc Joel Epstein, "The Third Force: Liberal Ideology in a Revolutionary Age, 1945–1950" (Ph.D. thesis, University of North Carolina, 1971); and Ronald Radosh, "The Economic and Political thought of Henry A. Wallace" (M.A. thesis, University of Iowa, 1960).
3. Henry A. Wallace, "I Shall Run in 1948," *Vital Speeches* 14 (January 1, 1948): 173.
4. Ibid.
5. Henry A. Wallace, "Stand Up and Be Counted," *New Republic* 168 (January 5, 1958): 5–10.
6. Lord, *The Wallaces of Iowa*, p. 569.
7. Barton J. Bernstein, "American Foreign Policy and the Origins of the Cold War," in *Politics and Policies of the Truman Administration*, ed. Barton J. Bernstein (Chicago: Quadrangle Books, 1970), p. 42. The italics are Bernstein's.

8. Ibid.
9. Wallace to Camacho, March 21, 1946, Wallace Papers.
10. Ibid.
11. Schapsmeier and Schapsmeier, *Prophet in Politics,* p. 145. The March 14, 1946, letter is printed in Truman, *Memoirs, I,* p. 555.
12. Hippelheuser, to Philip E. Hauser et al., July 17, 1946, Wallace Papers. Hauser was helping Wallace draft the letter. See Schapsmeier and Schapsmeier, *Prophet in Politics.*
13. Wallace to Truman, July 23, 1946. Alfred Schindler Papers, Harry S. Truman Library (hereafter cited as Schindler Papers). The letter was released September 17.
14. Ibid.   15. Ibid.   16. Ibid.
17. Truman to Wallace, August 8, 1946, Clark M. Clifford Papers, Harry S. Truman Library. The original draft read as follows: "Thank you for your long and thoughtful letter of July 23rd on the Russian problem. I agree with you that the question of our relations with the Soviet Union is one of the most important questions in the world today. I have been giving it a great deal of thought and I shall continue to do so."
18. Truman, *Memoirs, I,* pp. 556–557.
19. Interview with C. B. Baldwin, September 18, 1971.
20. Henry A. Wallace, "The Way to Peace," *Vital Speeches* 12 (October 1, 1946): 739.
21. Ibid.   22. Ibid., p. 740.   23. Ibid., p. 741.
24. Ibid., p. 740.   25. Ibid.
26. For an excellent detailed analysis of the events leading up to the speech and the aftermath, see Markowitz, "The Rise and Fall of the People's Century, pp. 374–393.
27. Wallace to Lawrence L. Persons, November 12, 1946, Wallace Papers.
28. Ibid.
29. Henry A. Wallace, *Toward World Peace* (New York: Reynal & Hitchcock, 1948), pp. 9–10.
30. Henry A. Wallace, "Henry Wallace Tells of His Political Odyssey," *Life* 40 (May 14, 1956): 178.
31. Truman, *Memoirs, I,* p. 557.
32. *Public Papers of the Presidents of the United States,* Harry S. Truman, 1946 (Washington, D.C.: Government Printing Office, 1962), pp. 426–427 (hereafter cited as *Public Papers,* 1946).
33. Ibid., p. 427, see the footnote.
34. "Statement by the President," September 14, 1946, Democratic National Committee Clipping File, Harry S. Truman Library. For a summary of newspaper opinion on Truman's actions, see the *St.*

Louis Post Dispatch, September 17, 1946, in the Democratic National Clipping File.

35. Ibid.
36. Henry A. Wallace statement, September 16, 1946, Schindler Papers.
37. L'Affaire Wallace, September 17, 1946, George M. Elsey Papers, Harry S. Truman Library.
38. Arthur H. Vandenberg, Jr., ed., *The Private Papers of Senator Vandenberg* (Boston: Houghton Mifflin, 1952), p. 302.
39. James F. Brynes, *Speaking Frankly* (New York: Harper and Brothers, 1947), p. 240.
40. Henry A. Wallace statement, September 18, 1946, Wallace Papers.
41. The president's statement may be found in the *Public Papers,* 1946, p. 431. Wallace's letter of resignation may be found in the Schindler Papers. The date is September 20, 1946.
42. Truman, *Memoirs, I,* p. 560.
43. Henry A. Wallace speech on the evening of September 20, 1946, Wallace Papers.
44. Interview with Michael Straight, April 1, 1971.
45. Murphy to Wallace, October 16, 1946, Wallace Papers.
46. Quoted in Schapsmeier and Schapsmeier, *Prophet in Politics,* p. 164.
47. Gilbert Harrison to Wallace, September 13, 1946, Wallace Papers.
48. Einstein to Wallace, September 18, 1946, Wallace Papers.
49. Ben Burns, executive editor of the *Negro Digest,* to Wallace, October 3, 1946, Wallace Papers.
50. Wallace to Lerner, September 28, 1946, Wallace Papers.
51. Wallace to Bruce, October 23, 1946, Wallace Papers.
52. Wallace to Robert G. Stuart, November 13, 1946, Wallace Papers.

CHAPTER II: 1947: AN EVENTFUL YEAR

1. Kenny to Paxton Haddow, October 10, 1946, Robert Kenny Papers, Bancroft Library, University of California, Berkeley. On reviewing this letter in a personal interview on March 12, 1972, Mr. Kenny, who is now a Superior Court judge in Los Angeles, said that the letter did reveal his feelings at the time. In 1948 Kenny headed a group called Democrats for Wallace, which he says did not really amount to much. For an account of Kenny's life, see his oral history memoir *My First Forty Years in California Politics, 1922–1962* (Los Angeles, 1964), Department of Special Collections, University of California at Los Angeles Library.
2. Wallace to Clemens, October 7, 1946, Wallace Papers. Claude Pepper, then Senator from Florida, was a severe critic of Administration foreign policy.
3. Wallace to Jake More, January 8, 1947, Wallace Papers.

4. Edward L. Schapsmeier and Frederick H. Schapsmeier, *Prophet in Politics: Henry A. Wallace and the War Years, 1940–1965* (Ames: Iowa State University Press, 1970), p. 166.

5. Interviews with Michael Straight, April 1, 1971, and C. B. Baldwin, September 18, 1971.

6. Quoted in a *New York Times* clipping, June 6, 1947, OF 299D, Harry S. Truman Papers, Harry S. Truman Library. See also Curtis D. MacDougall, *Gideon's Army*, I (New York: Marzani & Munsell, 1965), p. 164.

7. Quoted in William Hillman, *Mr. President* (New York: Farrar, Straus and Young, 1952), p. 128. Truman wrote this note to himself on September 19, 1946. He did not use Wallace's name, but there is no doubt about the fact that he was referring to him. That "X" was Wallace is now confirmed by Margaret Truman. See Margaret Truman, *Harry S. Truman* (New York: William Morrow, 1973), pp. 317–318.

8. *Public Papers of the Prsidents of the United States,* Harry S. Truman, 1947 (Washington, D.C.: Government Printing Office, 1963), pp. 176–180 (hereafter cited as *Public Papers*, 1947).

9. Quoted in MacDougall, *Gideon's Army*, p. 129. MacDougall says that the speech received very little coverage, and a check of the *New York Times* revealed a small article on page 7 of the March 14 edition.

10. Wallace's trip is covered in MacDougall, *Gideon's Army*, pp. 128–146. Wallace's reports of the trip appear in the *New Republic*. See Henry Wallace, "Report from Britain," *New Republic* 116 (April 28, 1947): 12–16; "Scandinavia-between Two Worlds" (May 5, 1947): 12–14; and "Report on France" (May 12, 1947): 12–15.

11. *Public Papers*, 1947, p. 203.

12. Clipping, *New York Times*, April 11, 1948, Democratic National Committee Clipping File, Harry S. Truman Library.

13. Harold Buchman to Wallace, March 15, 1947, Wallace Papers. Mr. Buchman was president of the Fourth District Roosevelt Democratic Club, Inc. of Baltimore, Maryland.

14. Herman Liveright to Wallace, August 26, 1947, American Labor Party Papers, Rutgers University Library. Mr. Liveright was executive director of the Westchester County branch of the American Labor party.

15. Clipping, April 18, 1947, Democratic National Committee Clipping File, Harry S. Truman Library.

16. Clark M. Clifford, "Memorandum For The President," November 19, 1947, Clark M. Clifford Papers, Harry S. Truman Library, p. 15.

17. Forrestal to Ross, March 28, 1947, OF 299D, Harry S. Truman Papers, Harry S. Truman Library.

18. Boykin to Truman, April 9, 1947, OF 1170, Harry S. Truman Papers, Harry S. Truman Library.

19. Ibid.

20. Truman to Boykin, April 11, 1947, OF 1170, Harry S. Truman Papers, Harry S. Truman Library.

21. Harry B. Hawes to Truman, April 19, 1947, OF 1170, Harry S. Truman Papers, Harry S. Truman Library.

22. Truman to Hawes, April 23, 1947, OF 1170, Harry S. Truman Papers, Harry S. Truman Library.

23. Starr to Truman, April 14, 1947, OF 1170, Harry S. Truman Papers, Harry S. Truman Library.

24. Truman to Starr, April 16, 1947, OF 1170, Harry S. Truman Papers, Harry S. Truman Library.

25. Clipping, May 28, 1947, Democratic National Committee Clipping File, Harry S. Truman Library. It is interesting to note that on May 28 Starr wrote to the president assuring him that he had not divulged to Allen or anybody else, the contents of the April 16 letter. See Starr to Truman, May 28, 1947, OF 1170, Harry S. Truman Papers, Harry S. Truman Library.

26. Elsey to Clifford, June 6, 1947, Clark M. Clifford Papers, Harry S. Truman Library.

27. Gael Sullivan, Memo re. Wallace Situation, June 2, 1947, Clark M. Clifford Papers, Harry S. Truman Library. The other item was an editorial from the June 2 edition of the *Washington Post*.

28. Ibid.   29. Ibid.   30. Ibid.

31. R. Alton Lee, *Truman and Taft-Hartley: A Question of Mandate* (Lexington: University of Kentucky Press, 1966), pp. 31–37. Truman's dealings with labor are also treated in Arthur F. McClure, *The Truman Administration and the Problems of Postwar Labor, 1945–1948* (Rutherford, Madison, Teaneck: Farleigh Dickinson University Press, 1969).

32. Lee, *Truman and Taft-Hartley*, p. 38.

33. *Time* 49 (June 30, 1947): 13.

34. Lee, *Truman and Taft-Hartley*, pp. 93–96.

35. Quoted in Lee, *Truman and Taft-Hartley*, p. 95. Lee quotes *Newsweek* 40 (June 23, 1947): 15 as the source.

36. Lee, *Truman and Taft-Hartley*, pp. 95–96. The Taft-Hartley veto is discussed in almost every source that covers the early Truman years in the presidency. The most recent is Susan M. Hartmann, *Truman and the 80th Congress* (Columbia: University of Missouri Press, 1971), pp. 87–88.

37. Henry Wallace, "The One Course to Save the Democratic Party" *New Republic* 117 (July 7, 1947): 14.

38. *Public Papers*, 1947, p. 297.

39. Irwin Ross, *The Loneliest Campaign: The Truman Victory of 1948* (New York: New American Library, 1968), p. 149.

40. MacDougall, *Gideon's Army*, p. 172.

41. Quoted in ibid., p. 178.

42. Ibid., p. 179.

43. Henry A. Wallace, "I Shall Run in 1948," *Vital Speeches* 14 (January 1, 1948): 174.

44. Roosevelt to McGrath, October 29, 1947, J. Howard McGrath Papers, Harry S. Truman Library. The bulk of the letter was concerned with Democratic party in-fighting in California. Copies of the letter were sent to Truman and Edwin Pauley. Pauley was the Democratic national committeeman from California.

45. Interview with C. B. Baldwin, September 18, 1971. Baldwin was the prime-mover in convincing Wallace to run. However, Wallace has said that he was unsure about running until "early December." He claimed that he decided to become a candidate in "late December." See Wallace to Fred Greenstein, January 11, 1953, Wallace Papers. The letter was never sent.

46. Interview with C. B. Baldwin, September 18, 1971.

47. MacDougall, *Gideon's Army*, p. 224.

48. Memorandum, December 2, 1947, Progressive Party Papers, University of Iowa Library. The entire memo is reprinted in ibid., pp. 225–226.

49. Ibid. and MacDougall, *Gideon's Army*, p. 225.

50. Douglas to Wallace, December 10, 1947, Progressive Party Papers, University of Iowa Library. Also see MacDougall, *Gideon's Army*, p. 242.

CHAPTER III: THE CLIFFORD MEMORANDUM ANALYZED

1. Oscar R. Ewing, Oral History Interview, April 30, May 1, and May 2, 1969. Harry S. Truman Library.

2. Cabell Phillips, *The Truman Presidency: The History of a Triumphant Succession* (New York: Macmillan, 1966), p. 162.

3. Interview with Clark M. Clifford, June 27, 1972.

4. Clifford quoted in Phillips, *The Truman Presidency*, pp. 163–164.

5. Interview with Clark M. Clifford, June 27, 1972.

6. Description is from an interview with Clark M. Clifford, June 27, 1972, and Irwin Ross, *The Loneliest Campaign: The Truman Victory of 1948* (New York: New American Library, 1968), pp. 20–21.

7. Ernest Havemann, "Clark Clifford," *Life* 22 (January 27, 1947): 45. The article in the *Saturday Evening Post* was Leigh White, "Truman's One-Man Brain Trust," 220 (October 4, 1947): 30–31, 106, 108, and 113.

8. Phillips, *The Truman Presidency,* p. 199.

9. Interview with George M. Elsey, July 2, 1971.

10. Interview with Clark M. Clifford, June 27, 1972.

11. Clark M. Clifford, "Memorandum For the President," November 19, 1947, Clark M. Clifford Papers, Harry S. Truman Library, p. 1 (hereafter cited as the Clifford Memorandum).

12. Ibid.   13. Ibid.   14. Ibid., p. 2.   15. Ibid., p. 3.

16. Interview with Clark M. Clifford, June 27, 1972.

17. Clifford Memorandum, p. 4.

18. Ibid.

19. The 1946 memorandum is reprinted in Arthur Krock, *Memoirs: Sixty Years on the Firing Line* (New York: Funk & Wagnalls, 1968), pp. 419–482. For a more perceptive analysis of Clifford's role in the formulation of the containment policy, see Richard J. Powers, "Who Fathered Containment?" *International Studies Quarterly* 15 (December 1971): 526–543.

20. Interview with Clark M. Clifford, June 27, 1972.

21. Clifford Memorandum, p. 4. Michael Straight, who was referred to by Clifford as one of the "gullible idealists" around Wallace, has denied that he ever pushed for a third party. Interview with Michael Straight, April 1, 1971.

22. Clifford Memorandum, p. 4.

23. Ibid., p. 5.   24. Ibid., p. 6.   25. Ibid.   26. Ibid.

27. Ibid., pp. 7–14.   28. Ibid., pp. 7–8.   29. Ibid., p. 8.

30. Ibid., p. 10.   31. Ibid., pp. 10–11.   32. Ibid., p. 11.

33. Ibid.   34. Ibid., pp. 12–13.

35. Wallace and Baldwin to Los Angeles County Office, Independent Progressive Party, November 4, 1948, Progressive Party Papers, University of Iowa Library.

36. Clifford Memorandum, p. 13.

37. Ibid.

38. Patrick Anderson, *The Presidents' Men* (Garden City: Doubleday, 1968), p. 118. On Truman and Israel, see Ian J. Bickerton, "President Truman's Recognition of Israel," *American Jewish Historical Quarterly* 58 (December 1968): 173–240.

39. Clifford Memorandum, p. 13.

40. Ibid., pp. 13–14.

41. Ibid., p. 14. In Clifford's words, "As of today the Administration enjoys good standing with the Harrison group interested in expanded immigration quotas. This is a result of the President's forthright fight for the Stratton Bill."

42. Ibid.   43. Ibid., p. 15.   44. Ibid.   45. Ibid., p. 17.

46. Ibid., p. 18.   47. Ibid., p. 19.   48. Ibid.   49. Ibid.

50. Ibid., p. 20.   51. Ibid., p. 21.   52. Ibid.   53. Ibid., p. 22.

54. Ibid., pp. 22–23.
55. Telephone conversation with Clark M. Clifford, July 2, 1971.
56. This topic is discussed in Chapter VI.
57. Clifford Memorandum, p. 23.
58. Ibid.   59. Ibid., p. 24.   60. Ibid.   61. Ibid., p. 25.
62. Ibid., pp. 25–29.   63. Ibid., p. 29.   64. Ibid.
65. Ibid., pp. 29–31.   66. Ibid., p. 30.   67. Ibid.   68. Ibid.
69. Ibid., p. 31.   70. Ibid., p. 32.   71. Ibid., p. 33.   72. Ibid.
73. Ibid.   74. Ibid., p. 35.
75. Richard O. Davies, *Housing Reform During the Truman Admin-istration* (Columbia: University of Missouri Press, 1966), p. 76.
76. Clifford Memorandum, p. 36.
77. Ibid., p. 37.   78. Ibid., p. 38.   79. Ibid., p. 39.   80. Ibid.
81. Ibid.   82. Ibid., p. 40.
83. Ibid. This came to be known as the research division of the Demo-cratic National Committee.
84. Ibid., pp. 40–41.
85. Ibid., pp. 41–42. Clifford called for this group to assemble "ma-terial for approximately ten major political speeches—the campaign speeches after the convention." However, the research division ended up working on much more than speeches.
86. Kenneth M. Birkhead.
87. Clifford Memorandum, p. 42.
88. Ibid., p. 43.

CHAPTER IV: REACTION

1. Brown to Connelly, December 29, 1947, OF 300, Harry S. Truman Papers, Harry S. Truman Library.
2. Henry A. Wallace, "I Shall Run in 1948," *Vital Speeches* 14 (Janu-ary 1, 1948): 173.
3. Quoted in Karl M. Schmidt, *Henry A. Wallace: Quixotic Crusade, 1948* (Syracuse: Syracuse University Press, 1960), pp. 39–40.
4. Wilson Wyatt quoted in *ADA World*, July 24, 1947, p. 1.
5. Max Lerner, "Wallace and 1948," *PM*, December 18, 1947, p. 12.
6. Max Lerner, "Wallace's Decision," *PM*, December 30, 1947, p. 10.
7. Ibid.
8. *New York Times*, December 30, 1947, p. 22.
9. *Nation* 166 (January 3, 1948): 1, and *Nation* 166 (January 10, 1948): 29–31.
10. *Washington Post*, December 29, 1947, p. 6.
11. Curtis D. MacDougall, *Gideon's Army*, I (New York: Marzani & Munsell, 1965), p. 286. MacDougall should also be consulted for his coverage of the reaction to the Wallace announcement. See Volume I, "Announcement and Reaction," pp. 284–305.

12. Edward T. Folliard, "Somebody Errs About Gideon's Army," *Washington Post,* January 4, 1948, pp. 1b and 8b.

13. Ibid., p. 1b. Brown, who was Robert Taft's campaign manager, was quoted by Folliard.

14. Ibid., p. 8b.

15. *Public Papers,* 1947, p. 536.

16. Robert F. Wagner, December 29, 1947, and Truman to Wagner, OF 1170, Harry S. Truman Papers, Harry S. Truman Library. Wagner's career is treated by J. Joseph Huthmacher, *Senator Robert F. Wagner and the Rise of Urban Liberalism* (New York: Atheneum, 1971). For Wagner on Wallace, see page 316.

17. McCormack quoted in Folliard, "Somebody Errs About Gideon's Army, p. 1b.

18. Lucas quoted in *Time* 51 (January 12, 1948): 12.

19. Ibid.

20. McGrath quoted in *Capitol Comment,* January 3, 1948, American Labor Party Papers, Box A-E, Democratic Party folder, Rutgers University Library.

21. Ibid.

22. McNaughton to Don Bermingham, January 2, 1948, Frank McNaughton Papers, Harry S. Truman Library.

23 Ibid.   24. Ibid.   25. Ibid.

26. Ibid.

27. This election is discussed in Alonzo Hamby, "Harry S. Truman and American Liberalism, 1945–1948" (Ph.D. thesis, University of Missouri, 1965), pp. 217–219; MacDougall, *Gideon's Army,* II, pp. 323–326; and Schmidt, *Harry A. Wallace: Quixotic Crusade,* pp. 67–71.

28. Quoted in MacDougall, *Gideon's Army,* II, p. 324.

29. Hamby, "Harry S. Truman and American Liberalism," p. 218.

30. *Nation* 166 (February 14, 1948): 171.

31. Ibid.

32. MacDougall, *Gideon's Army,* II, p. 325.

33. Propper, 12,578; Alfange, 3,840; DeNigris, 1,482.

34. Quoted in *Washington Post,* February 18, 1948, p. 1.

35. Frank Ross Peterson, "Liberal From Idaho: The Public Career of Senator Glen H. Taylor" (Ph.D. thesis, Washington State University, 1968), p. 145.

36. *Time* 51 (March 1, 1948): 13.

37. Flynn quoted in *Washington Post,* February 18, 1948, p. 2.

38. McGrath quoted in *Washington Post,* February 19, 1948, p. 2.

39. Newspaper clippings, Progressive Party Papers, University of Iowa Library.

40. Ibid.

41. McCormack and Bowles quoted in *Washington Post*, February 19, 1948, p. 2.
42. Wyatt quoted in ibid.
43. Max Lerner, "The Lesson of the Isacson Victory," *PM*, February 19, 1948, p. 1.
44. Moscow is quoted in Schmidt, *Henry A. Wallace: Quixotic Crusade*, p. 70.
45. Gus Tyler, "Memorandum on the Recent Election in the 24th Congressional District, Bronx, New York," n.d., Americans for Democratic Action Papers, State Historical Society of Wisconsin. Tyler worked on the memorandum by himself and then circulated it to a small group of people. Interview with Gus Tyler, June 30, 1972.
46. Ibid.   47. Ibid.
48. Newspaper clipping, February 24, 1948, OF 299D, Harry S. Truman Papers, Harry S. Truman Library.
49. Ibid.   50. Ibid.
51. *News, Liberal Party*, February 10, 1948, Progressive Party Papers, University of Iowa.
52. Alfange quoted in MacDougall, *Gideon's Army*, II, pp. 845–846.
53. Berle quoted in *News, Liberal Party*, February 16, 1948, Progressive Party Papers, University of Iowa Library.
54. Ibid.
55. *Public Papers*, 1948, p. 105.
56. Ibid., p. 189.
57. Newspaper Clippings, Clipping File, Democratic National Committee, Harry S. Truman Library.
58. Elsey to Clifford, March 5, 1948. George M. Elsey Papers, Harry S. Truman Library.
59. Ibid.
60. *Public Papers*, 1948, p. 185.
61. "Speech by H. A. Wallace," Minneapolis, Minnesota, February 27, 1948, Henry A. Wallace Papers, University of Iowa Library. Also see MacDougall, *Gideon's Army*, II, pp. 332–333.
62. MacDougall, *Gideon's Army*, II, p. 334.
63. *Washington Post*, March 20, 1948, p. 6.
64. Crowd reaction is mentioned by *New York Times* reporter Frank S. Adams in his article "Truman Rejects Any Backing of Wallace and Communists," *New York Times*, March 18, 1948, Democratic National Committee Clipping File, Harry S. Truman Library.
65. Wallace quoted in MacDougall, *Gideon's Army*, II, p. 339.
66. Henry A. Wallace over NBC, March 26, 1948, Henry A. Wallace Papers, University of Iowa Library. Also see MacDougall, *Gideon's Army*, II, pp. 340–341.

67. According to the George Gallup American Institute of Public Opinion Poll, as of February 29, 1948, Wallace was going to receive 15 percent of New York's vote, 7 percent of Pennsylvania's, 8 percent of Illinois's and 11 percent of California's. See *Public Opinion Quarterly* 12 (Summer 1948): 361.
68. McNaughton to Don Bermingham, March 19, 1948, Frank McNaughton Papers, Harry S. Truman Library.
69. Ibid.   70. Ibid.   71. Ibid.   72. Ibid.

CHAPTER V: ISSUES OF THE CAMPAIGN

1. Wallace to Stanley J. Beyer, November 29, 1948, Wallace Papers.
2. Frank Ross Peterson, "Liberal from Idaho: The Public Career of Senator Glen H. Taylor" (Ph.D. diss. Washington State University, 1968), p. 189. Peterson cites an interview that he had with Taylor on June 14, 1967.
3. Interview for Curtis D. MacDougall with Claude Pepper, early March 1953, Progressive Party Papers, University of Iowa Library (hereafter cited as Progressive Party Papers).
4. Ibid.
5. Walter LaFeber, *America, Russia, and the Cold War, 1945–1971* (New York: John Wiley, 1967, 1972), p. 72.
6. Paul Y. Hammond, *The Cold War Years: American Foreign Policy Since 1945* (New York: Harcourt, Brace & World, 1969), pp. 33–34.
7. Richard S. Kirkendall, "Election of 1948," in *History of American Presidential Elections*, IV, ed. Arthur M. Schlesinger (New York: Chelsea House, 1971), p. 3136.
8. Even Karl Schmidt grants this point. See Karl M. Schmidt, *Henry A. Wallace: Quixotic Crusade, 1948* (Syracuse: Syracuse University Press, 1960), p. 318.
9. Wallace to J. G. Couser, May 11, 1948, Wallace Papers. While Wallace's name did not appear on the draft, the letter was written in the first person and was obviously very carefully worked out for him by Progressive strategists.
10. Ibid. Along with repeal of Taft-Hartley, Wallace wanted higher wages with extensive government planning, old age pensions, an end to segregation, the establishment of a permanent FEPC, and a crash housing program.
11. Ibid.   12. Ibid.
13. "Why Third Party," Progressive Papers. This speech was written sometime between May and the Democratic Convention (July 12).
14. Ibid.   15. Ibid.   16. Ibid.   17. Ibid.   18. Ibid.
19. Ibid.   20. Ibid.   21. Ibid.   22. Ibid.
23. Quoted in Kirk H. Porter and Donald Bruce Johnson, comps., *Na-*

tional Party Platforms, 1840–1964 (Urbana: University of Illinois Press, 1966), p. 436.

24. Ibid.   25. Ibid., p. 437.   26. Ibid.   27. Ibid.
28. Ibid.   29. Ibid., p. 438.   30. Ibid., pp. 441–447.
31. Ibid., p. 438.
32. Interview with Clark M. Clifford, June 27, 1972, and "Memorandum For The President," November 19, 1947, Clark M. Clifford Papers, Harry S. Truman Library (hereafter cited as Clifford Papers). Other advisors who favored using the State of the Union address were Charles S. Murphy and George M. Elsey. Murphy is briefly discussed in Susan M. Hartmann, *Truman and the 80th Congress* (Columbia: University of Missouri Press, 1971), p. 130, while Elsey is mentioned in Irwin Ross, *The Loneliest Campaign: The Truman Victory of 1948* (New York: New American Library, 1968), pp. 55–56. In personal interviews with both of these men on July 2, 1971, neither mentioned their roles with respect to advice on the State of the Union.
33. *Public Papers,* 1948, p. 3.
34. Ibid.   35. Ibid., pp. 3–4.   36. Ibid., p. 3.
37. The State of the Union Message is interpreted differently in Ross, *The Loneliest Campaign,* pp. 56–58.
38. *Public Papers,* 1948, pp. 4–5.
39. Ibid., p. 6.   40. Ibid., p. 8.
41. Ibid., pp. 9–10. The *New York Times* was generally favorable toward the speech with the exception of this last point. In an editorial entitled "The President's Tax Plan," the paper attacked the plan as part of "election year maneuvering." *New York Times,* January 8, 1948, p. 24. For some other comment on the speech, see Ross, *The Loneliest Campaign,* pp. 59–60.
42. Richard O. Davies, "Social Welfare Policies," in *The Truman Period as a Research Field* ed. Richard Kirkendall (Columbia: University of Missouri Press, 1967), p. 176.
43. Ross, *The Loneliest Campaign,* pp. 57–58.
44. Barton J. Bernstein, ed., "The Ambiguous Legacy: The Truman Administration and Civil Rights," in *Politics and Policies of the Truman Administration,* ed. Barton J. Bernsten (Chicago: Quadrangle Books, 1970), p. 282.
45. William C. Berman, *The Politics of Civil Rights in the Truman Administration* (Columbus: Ohio State University Press, 1970), p. 83. More evidence for this point of view is supplied by Philip H. Vaughan who quotes George Elsey writing the following to Clifford: "Elsey's note stated that 'proper handling' of the civil rights issue could 'virtually assure the election of the President by cutting the

ground out from under Wallace and gaining the enthusiastic support of the liberal and labor groups.'" See Philip H. Vaughan, "President Truman's Committee on Civil Rights: The Urban Implications," *Missouri Historical Review* 66 (April 1972): 427.

46. Memorandum, "A Minimum Civil Rights Program for the Eightieth Congress," January 8, 1948, Philleo Nash Papers, Harry S. Truman Library. I assume the memorandum was prepared by Nash.

47. On this topic, see Berman, *The Politics of Civil Rights*, pp. 82–85. The message is in *Public Papers*, 1948, pp. 125–126.

48. Clark M. Clifford, "Memorandum for the President," November 19, 1947, Clifford Papers, p. 12.

49. Batt to Sullivan, April 20, 1948, Clifford Papers. The first paragraph of the memo read as follows: "Jack Ewing last night gave us a shocking report on the Negro vote in New York City. I had seen polls to the effect that from 20% to 30% of the Negro voters were going to vote for Wallace, but he reported interviews with what he said were the two best ward leaders in Harlem and Brooklyn, both of whom said that about 75% of their voters were going to vote for Wallace."

50. Alexander to Batt, Jr., April 5, 1948, Philleo Nash Files, Harry S. Truman Library.

51. Alexander to Myers, May 11, 1948, J. Howard McGrath Papers, Harry S. Truman Library.

52. Batt to Clifford, August 11, 1948, and Clifford to the President, August 17, 1948, Clifford Papers.

53. William L. Batt, Jr., Oral History Interview, July 26, 1966, p. 16. Harry S. Truman Library.

54. Interview with William L. Batt, Jr., July 2, 1971.

55. Kenneth M. Birkhead, Oral History Interview, July 7, 1966, pp. 2 and 6, Harry S. Truman Library.

56. Ibid., p. 6.   57. Ibid., p. 22.

58. Batt to Clifford, August 11, 1948, and Clark M. Clifford to the President, August 17, 1948, Clifford Papers.

59. Memorandum, Summaries of the President's campaign speeches, Harlem, N.Y., October 29, Clifford Papers. These summaries begin on June 4 and go through November 1. This was number 286.

60. Quoted in Porter and Johnson, comps., *National Party Platforms*, p. 435.

61. Ross, *The Loneliest Campaign*, pp. 120-125. William Berman also discusses the civil rights plank in his work. See Berman, *The Politics of Civil Rights*, pp. 106–113. Ross's statement is supported by former Washington State Congressman Hugh Mitchell, who has said that the civil rights plank had to be thrust upon Truman. Interview with Hugh B. Mitchell and the late Harold Tipton,

November 30, 1967. Tipton had been Mitchell's campaign manager and later managed the senatorial campaign of Helen Gahagan
Douglas against Richard M. Nixon. The transcript of this interview
is now in the manuscript division of the University of Washington
Library.

62. Harry S. Truman, *Memoirs,* II New York: Doubleday, 1956), p.
246.

63. LaFeber, *America, Russia, and the Cold War, 1945–1971,* pp. 63–64.
A very recent article that perceptively treats foreign policy in the
1948 campaign is Robert A. Divine, "The Cold War and the Election of 1948," *Journal of American History* 59 (June 1972): 90–110.

64. Richard M. Freeland, *The Truman Doctrine and the Origins of
McCarthyism* (New York: Alfred A. Knopf, 1972), p. 5.

65. *Time,* 51 (April 12, 1948), p. 23.

66. *New York Times,* March 30, 1948, p. 1.

67. Batt to McGrath and Redding, June 21, 1948, Clifford Papers.

68. Ibid.

69. Quoted in Porter and Johnson, comps., *National Party Platforms,*
pp. 431–432.

70. Batt to Clifford, July 9, 1948, Charles S. Murphy Files, Harry S.
Truman Library. A draft of a speech was enclosed with this memo
but it was not used.

71. *Public Papers,* 1948, p. 407.

72. Ibid.

73. After his discussion of foreign policy, the president launched into
Congressional Republicans hitting at their lack of domestic achieve-
ment. The highlight of the speech came when he announced that
he was calling the Congress back into special session on July 26. On
this specific topic one can consult the unsigned memorandum dated
June 29, 1948, in the Samuel Rosenman papers at the Harry S. Truman Library. Its title is "Should the President call Congress back?"
and Mr. Rosenman has said that although it is in his papers, he did
not write it. See Samuel I. Rosenman, Oral History Interview,
October 15, 1968, and April 23, 1969, p. 32, Harry S. Truman
Library. The mystery as to who authored this specific document
still goes on. The document is reproduced in Barton J. Bernstein
and Allen J. Matusow, eds., *The Truman Administration: A Documentary History* (New York: Harper & Row, 1966), pp. 147–150.

74. Curtis D. MacDougall, *Gideon's Army,* II (New York: Marzani &
Munsell, 1965), pp. 351–355. Wallace has identified Anita Blaine as
the person responsible for the open letter. See Wallace to Fred
Greenstein, January 11, 1953, Wallace Papers. This letter was not
sent.

75. Schmidt, *Henry A. Wallace: Quixotic Crusade,* p. 78.

76. Truman, *Memoirs,* II, p. 213. Truman's explanation of the episode places little emphasis on the Progressives. He discusses the whole matter on pp. 212–219.
77. Elsey to Clifford, August 26, 1948, George M. Elsey Papers, Harry S. Truman Library.
78. *Public Papers,* 1948, pp. 558–559. Alan Harper also treats this speech. See Alan Harper, *The Politics of Loyalty: The White House and the Communist Issue, 1946–1962* (Westport: Greenwood Publishing Company, 1969), pp. 76–78.
79. Batt to Murphy, September 13, 1948, Clifford Papers. The subject of the memo was the *"President's Speech in Los Angeles."*
80. Ibid.   81. Ibid.   82. Ibid.   83. Ibid.   84. Ibid.
85. Carr to Connelly, Clifford Papers. No date is given, but I believe it is September 22.
86. Ibid. On the day of the California speech, Charles Murphy sent a message to Matt Connelly praising the work of Carr saying that "I think Bob Carr is the best we have had and the best we are likely to have at writing speeches. Please send him some encouraging word." On the matter of the Progressives, Murphy recommended that Truman inform the "liberals" that they "will be wasting their vote if they vote for the Third Party." See Murphy to Connelly, September 23, 1948, Charles S. Murphy Files, Harry S. Truman Library.
87. Batt to Clark M. Clifford, September 14, 1948, Clifford Papers.
88. Interview with Stephen J. Spingarn, July 3, 1971.
89. Spingarn to Clifford, September 18, 1948, Stephen J. Spingarn Papers, Harry S. Truman Library.
90. Interview with Stephen J. Spingarn, July 3, 1971.
91. *Public Papers,* 1948, p. 610.
92. Harper, *The Politics of Loyalty,* p. 82.
93. John Franklin Carter, Oral History Interview, October 7, 1966, p. 6, Harry S. Truman Library. The sentence quoted was read by the interviewer.
94. Rosenman to Truman, October 26, 1948, Samuel I. Rosenman papers, Harry S. Truman Library.
95. *Public Papers,* 1948, pp. 884 and 929.
96. Interview by Mrs. Norman Sun for Curtis MacDougall, with Harry S. Truman, May 26, 1953, Progressive Party Papers.
97. Batt to Clifford, August 11, 1948, Clifford Papers.
98. Clifford to the President, August 17, 1948, Clifford Papers.

CHAPTER VI: LIBERALS AND 1948

1. By 1947 Philip Murray had purged the CIO of Communists, and the liberal anti-Communist line had already taken hold. For an account

of a former member of the CIO who was "purged," see Len DeCaux, *Labor Radical* Boston: Beacon Press, 1970), pp. 470–485.

2. Thomas to Professor and Mrs. Edward S. Allen, June 28, 1948, Norman Thomas Papers, New York Public Library.

3. See Murray B. Seidler, *Norman Thomas: Respectable Rebel* (Syracuse: Syracuse University Press, 1961), p. 231, and Bernard K. Johnpoll, *Pacifist's Progress: Norman Thomas and the Decline of American Socialism* (Chicago: Quadrangle Books, 1970) for the most recent account of Thomas' life.

4. James Loeb, Jr., "Progressives and Communists," *New Republic* 114 (May 13, 1946): 699. Two accounts that treat the letter, and the commotion that it created, are Clifton Brock, *Americans for Democratic Action: Its Role in National Politics* (Washington, D.C.: Public Affairs Press, 1962), pp. 46, 49–50, and Curtis D. Mac-Dougall, *Gideon's Army*, I (New York: Marzani & Munsell, 1965), pp. 123–124.

5. Stanley M. Isaacs, "Progressives and Communists," *New Republic* 114 (May 20, 1946): 733.

6. Interview with Michael Straight, April 1, 1971.

7. The formation of the ADA and PCA is treated in Brock, *Americans for Democratic Action*, ch. IV, and MacDougall, *Gideon's Army*, I, ch. VI.

8. Quoted in Brock, *Americans for Democratic Action*, p. 52.

9. Quoted in Joseph P. Lash, *Eleanor: The Years Alone* (New York: W.W. Norton, 1972), p. 93.

10. Henry A. Wallace, "Report from Britain," *New Republic* 116 (April 28, 1947): 116.

11. *ADA World*, April 26, 1947, p. 2. The editorial was entitled "The Wallace Episode."

12. *ADA World*, June 18, 1947, p. 1.

13. "Liberalism," Wallace Papers. A revised version of this article appeared in the *New York Times Magazine*, April 18, 1948, under Wallace's name.

14. Wilson W. Wyatt, "Creed for Liberals: A Ten Point Program," *New York Times Magazine*, July 27, 1947, pp. 7, 35–36.

15. Quoted in ibid., p. 36.

16. Ibid., p. 37.

17. Ibid.

18. Quoted in *ADA World*, July 24, 1947, p. 1.

19. Henry A. Wallace, "I Shall Run in 1948," *Vital Speeches*, 14 (January 1, 1948): 174.

20. Loeb to Otto L. Spaeth, January 14, 1948, Americans for Democratic Action Papers, State Historical Society of Wisconsin (hereafter cited as ADA Papers).

21. Loeb to Albert Sprague Coolidge, January 22, 1948, ADA Papers. Coolidge was a socialist.
22. Tugwell to Henderson, January 29, 1948, ADA Papers. Leon Henderson became National Chairman of the ADA in 1948. Tugwell's letter was addressed to Henderson as chairman of the Executive Committee.
23. Rexford G. Tugwell, "Progressives and the Presidency," *The Progressive* 13 (April 1949): 5.
24. Ibid.　　　　25. Ibid.
26. Interview with Rexford G. Tugwell, July 22, 1971.
27. Hubert Humphrey, "A Reply to Rex Tugwell," *The Progressive* 13 (April 1949): 7.
28. Humphrey to Loeb, Jr., March 24, 1948, ADA Papers.
29. Humphrey to Loeb, Jr., April 27, 1948, ADA Papers.
30. George Demetriou to Wechsler, March 24, 1948, ADA Papers. Wechsler helped to write material for the ADA.
31. Arthur M. Schlesinger, Jr., *The Vital Center: The Politics of Freedom* (Boston: Houghton Mifflin, 1949), p. 116. The 1962 paperback edition was used for this study.
32. Loeb to Executive Committee, March 16, 1948, ADA Papers.
33. Dr. Johannes Hoeber, Oral History Interview, September 13, 1966, Harry S. Truman Library, p. 22.
34. Loeb to author, July 21, 1971, and Rauh, Jr. to author, July 28, 1971. Rauh was chairman of the Executive Committee in 1948.
35. Interview with William Batt, Jr., July 2, 1971. Batt made the point that the ADA had opposed Truman for a time, and an agreement would have had to have been made after the group began to support the president. By this time the ADA was already heavily involved in its anti-Wallace campaign.
36. Interview with Clark M. Clifford, June 27, 1972. Clifford was, of course, correct. For evidence, see Memorandum Re Conversation with Walter Reuther, March 15, 1948, and Memorandum on Conversation with David Dubinsky, March 15, 1948, ADA Papers. Both of these labor leaders wanted someone other than Truman as the Democratic candidate.
37. In the Truman Library there is a note from Gael Sullivan to J. Howard McGrath which deals with a meeting with Leon Henderson. Sullivan to McGrath, January 27, 1948, J. Howard McGrath Papers, Harry S. Truman Library. Sullivan wrote "I thought it better to spell out certain points of discussion for the ADA meeting." Sullivan's agenda consisted of three points, one of which was "Active use of the organization to aid the Democratic cause." See Sullivan to Paul Porter, January 27, 1948, J. Howard McGrath Papers, Harry S. Truman Library.

38. Henderson to Dear PAC Friend, April 28, 1948, ADA Papers.
39. *Henry A. Wallace: The First Three Months,* ADA Papers, p. 1.
40. Ibid., pp. 1–2.   41. Ibid., p. 2.   42. Ibid., p. 5.
43. Ibid., p. 7.   44. Ibid., p. 12.   45. Ibid., p. 15.
46. Ibid., pp. 18–19.   47. Ibid., p. 20.   48. Ibid., p. 28.
49. Ibid., p. 33.   50. Ibid., p. 24.   51. Ibid., p. 30.
52. Wyatt to Rauh, Jr., May 3, 1948, ADA Papers.
53. Schlesinger, *The Vital Center,* p. 264. However, he did write they were "critical memoranda."
54. This was verified when Professor Schlesinger served as one of the critics on an earlier version of this chapter presented at the American Historical Association meeting, December 29, 1971.
55. MacDougall, *Gideon's Army,* III, p. 639.
56. Wallace to Anita McCormick Blaine, April 2, 1948, Wallace Papers. Other than his speeches one can also find Wallace's views in his book, *Toward World Peace* (New York: Reynal and Hitchcock, 1948).
57. Wallace to Alfred Kohlberg, September 9, 1952, Wallace Papers. Wallace incorrectly recalled that his remarks were made in the fall. The *New York Times* reported the episode on page 16 of its July 3, 1948, issue. For an account of the Center Sandwich episode, see MacDougall, *Gideon's Army,* II, pp. 426–427.
58. The appearance is treated in Brock, *Americans for Democratic Action,* pp. 76–78, and MacDougall, *Gideon's Army,* II, pp. 549–553.
59. Loeb to Mrs. J. G. Schutte, July 27, 1948, ADA Papers.
60. Whitney to Henderson, August 5, 1948, ADA Papers.
61. Quoted in Robert Sam Anson, *McGovern: A Biography* (New York: Holt, Rinehart and Winston, 1972), p. 60. According to Anson, while McGovern supported Wallace, he became disillusioned with the movement and did not vote on election day. See page 61.
62. Rauh, to Loeb, September 3, 1948, ADA Papers.
63. Loeb, to Niebuhr, September 17, 1948, ADA Papers. Loeb had already outlined his ideas to Niebuhr on the phone. On September 30, he thanked Niebuhr for his help on the project. See Loeb to Niebuhr, September 30, 1948, ADA Papers.
64. "An Appeal to the Liberals of America," ADA Papers.
65. Loeb to Neibuhr, September 17, 1948, ADA Papers.
66. *Henry A. Wallace: The Last Seven Months of His Presidential Campaign,* ADA Papers, p. 32.
67. Ibid.   68. Ibid., p. 33.
69. Brock, *Americans for Democratic Action,* p. 81.
70. MacDougall, *Gideon's Army,* III, p. 639.
71. Robert Griffith, *The Politics of Fear: Joseph R. McCarthy and the Senate* (Lexington: University of Kentucky Press, 1970), p. 46.

72. Athan Theoharis, "The Rhetoric of Politics: Foreign Policy, Internal Security, and Domestic Politics in the Truman Era, 1945–1950," in *Politics and Policies of the Truman Administration*, ed. Barton J. Bernstein (Chicago: Quadrangle Books, 1970), p. 221.

CHAPTER VII: END RESULTS

1. Probably the most famous political photograph of recent times is the one showing a beaming Harry Truman holding a copy of the *Chicago Tribune* with a headline stating "Dewey Defeats Truman."

2. Richard M. Scammon, ed., *American at the Polls* (Pittsburgh: University of Pittsburgh Press, 1965), pp. 15–16. They were, however, important in the states of New York and Michigan where they probably lost the state for Truman to Dewey.

3. Angus Campbell, Philip E. Converse, Warren E. Miller, and Donald E. Stokes, *The American Voter: An Abridgement* (New York: John Wiley, 1964), p. 275.

4. Samuel Lubell, *The Future of American Politics*, 3rd ed., rev. (New York: Harper & Row, 1965), pp. 200–204.

5. Ibid., p. 203.   6. Ibid., p. 201.

7. Wallace to Truman, November 5, 1948, PPF 1917, Harry S. Truman Papers, Harry S. Truman Library. See also Curtis MacDougall, *Gideon's Army*, III (New York: Marzani & Munsell), pp. 883–884.

8. Ibid.   9. Ibid.

10. Tugwell to Ross, November 15, 1948, OF, 394, Harry S. Truman Papers, Harry S. Truman Library.

11. Ibid. The idea of a mission headed by Vinson had been brought up during the campaign but had been dropped.

12. One must remember that Tugwell still maintains that Progressives had a positive impact on Truman and the Democrats. Interview with Rexford Tugwell, July 22, 1971.

13. Lubell, *The Future of American Politics*, p. 200; Walter Johnson, *1600 Pennsylvania Avenue* (Boston: Little, Brown, 1963), pp. 232–233; and Irwin Ross, *The Loneliest Campaign: The Truman Victory of 1948* (New York: New American Library, 1968), p. 253.

14. MacDougall, *Gideon's Army*, III, pp. 860–863 and interviews with Beanie Baldwin, September 18, 1971; Len DeCaux, July 21, 1971; and Rexford Tugwell, July 22, 1971.

15. *New York Star*, November 4, 1948, p. 14.

16. Ibid.

17. *New York Times*, November 4, 1948, p. 28.

18. *Time* 52 (November 8, 1948): 21.

19. "Statement by Henry A. Wallace," November 3, 1948, Wallace Papers.

20. Wallace to Anita Blaine, November 9, 1948, Wallace Papers.

21. Wallace to James Crutchfield, November 10, 1948, and Wallace to Alfred Drake, November 10, 1948, Wallace Papers.
22. "Personal Statement by Henry A. Wallace on the Korean Situation," July 15, 1950, and Wallace to Beanie Baldwin, August 8, 1948, for the resignation, Wallace Papers.
23. Pepper to Wallace, July 26, 1950, Wallace Papers.
24. Wallace to Pepper, August 8, 1950, Wallace Papers.
25. Humphrey to Wallace, February 16, 1951, Wallace Papers.
26. Wallace to David Batten, January 1, 1957, Wallace Papers. Wallace's public statement on this can be found in Henry A. Wallace, "Henry Wallace Tells of His Political Odyssey," *Life* 40 (May 14, 1956): 174–190.
27. Wallace to MacDougall, August 5, 1953, Wallace Papers.
28. John E. Barriere, Oral History Interview, December 20, 1966, p. 7, Harry S. Truman Library.

—

BIBLIOGRAPHY

I. UNPUBLISHED SOURCES

A. Manuscript Collections

Americans for Democratic Action. State Historical Society of Wisconsin.
American Labor Party. Rutgers University.
Alben Barkley. University of Kentucky.
Naomi Benson. University of Washington.
Gus Carlson. University of Washington.
Oscar L. Chapman. Harry S. Truman Library.
Clark M. Clifford. Harry S. Truman Library.
Jo Davidson. Library of Congress.
Democratic National Committee Clipping File. Harry S. Truman Library.
George M. Elsey. Harry S. Truman Library.
Dwight D. Eisenhower. Dwight D. Eisenhower Library.
Leonard Finder. Dwight D. Eisenhower Library.
James V. Forrestal. Princeton University Library.
Robert W. Kenny. Bancroft Library, University of California, Berkeley.
Harley M. Kilgore. Franklin D. Roosevelt Library.
Jack Kroll. Library of Congress.
David Lloyd. Harry S. Truman Library.
Ruth Lybeck. University of California, Los Angeles.
J. Howard McGrath. Harry S. Truman Library.
Frank McNaughton. Harry S. Truman Library.
Vito Marcantonio. New York Public Library.
Hugh B. Mitchell. University of Washington.
Charles S. Murphy. Harry S. Truman Library.
Philleo Nash. Harry S. Truman Library.
Progressive Party Papers. University of Iowa.
John M. Redding. Harry S. Truman Library.
Samuel I. Rosenman. Harry S. Truman Library.
Charles G. Ross. Harry S. Truman Library.
Alfred Schindler. Harry S. Truman Library.
Stephen J. Spingarn. Harry S. Truman Library.
Genevieve Fallon Steefel. Library of Congress.
Elbert D. Thomas. Franklin D. Roosevelt Library.
Norman Thomas. New York Public Library.

Harry S. Truman. General File. Harry S. Truman Library.
————. Official File. Harry S. Truman Library.
————. President's Personal File. Harry S. Truman Library.
Henry A. Wallace. University of Iowa.
Washington Pension Union. University of Washington.
Aubrey Williams. Franklin D. Roosevelt Library.

B. Interviews

C. B. "Beanie" Baldwin (with author). September 18, 1971.
John E. Barriere. December 20, 1966. Harry S. Truman Library.
William L. Batt. July 26, 1966. Harry S. Truman Library.
———— (with author). July 2, 1971.
Kenneth M. Birkhead. July 7, 1966. Harry S. Truman Library.
Samuel C. Brightman. December 7–8, 1966. Harry S. Truman Library.
John Franklin Carter. October 7, 1966. Harry S. Truman Library.
Clark M. Clifford (with author). June 27, 1972.
Jonathan Daniels. October 4–5, 1966. Harry S. Truman Library.
Len DeCaux (with author). July 21, 1971.
George M. Elsey (with author). July 2, 1971.
Oscar R. Ewing. April 30–May 1–2, 1969. Harry S. Truman Library.
Johannes Hoeber. September 13, 1966. Harry S. Truman Library.
Robert W. Kenny. 1969, University of California, Los Angeles.
———— (with author). March 12, 1972.
Thomas Lynch (with author). November 7, 1967. University of Washington.
Carey McWilliams (with author). June 30, 1972.
Hugh B. Mitchell (with author). November 30, 1967. University of Washington.
Charles S. Murphy. May 2, 1963. Harry S. Truman Library.
———— (with author). July 2, 1971.
Terry Pettus (with author). February 1, 1967. University of Washington.
Samuel I. Rosenman. October 15, 1968, and April 23, 1969. Harry S. Truman Library.
Arthur M. Schlesinger, Jr. (with author). April 3, 1968.
Stephen J. Spingarn (with author). July 3, 1971.
Joseph Starobin (with author). May 10, 1972.
Michael Straight (with author). April 1, 1971.
Peter Tager (with author). July 22, 1971.
Norman Thomas. 1950. Columbia University Oral History Collection.
Rexford G. Tugwell (with author). July 22, 1971.
Gus Tyler (with author). June 30, 1972.

C. Personal Correspondence

James I. Loeb to author, July 21, 1971.
Joseph L. Rauh, Jr. to author, July 28, 1971.

D. Theses

Barto, Harold. "Clark Clifford and the Presidential Election of 1948." Ph.D. thesis, Rutgers University, 1970.

Binter, John Stuart. "Clark Clifford and the 1948 Election." M.A. thesis, University of Missouri, Kansas City, 1969.

Devita. Virginio Francis. "The Americans for Democratic Action and Harry S. Truman, 1945–1948." M.A. thesis, University of Wisconsin, 1962.

Epstein, Marc Joel. "The Third Force: Liberal Ideology in a Revolutionary Age, 1945–1950." Ph.D. thesis, University of North Carolina, 1971.

Hamby, Alonzo L. "Harry S. Truman and American Liberalism, 1945–1948." Ph.D. thesis, University of Missouri, 1965.

Hinchey, Mary Hedge. "The Frustration of the New Deal Revival, 1944–1946." Ph.D. thesis, University of Missouri, 1965.

Markowitz, Norman. "The Rise and Fall of the People's Century: Henry Agard Wallace and American Liberalism, 1941–1948." Ph.D. thesis, University of Michigan, 1970.

Peterson, Frank Ross. "Liberal from Idaho: The Public Career of Senator Glen H. Taylor." Ph.D. thesis, Washington State University, 1968.

Prickett, James Robert. "The Communist Controversy in the CIO." M.A. thesis, San Diego State College, 1969.

Pritchard, Robert Louis. "Southern Politics and the Truman Administration: Georgia as a Test Case." Ph.D. thesis, University of California, Los Angeles, 1970.

Radosh, Ronald. "The Economic and Political Thought of Henry A. Wallace." M.A. thesis, University of Iowa, 1960.

Wallace, Harold Lew. "The Campaign of 1948." Ph.D. thesis, Indiana University, 1970.

II. PUBLISHED SOURCES

A. Articles

Berman, William C. "Civil Rights and Civil Liberties." In *The Truman Administration as a Research Field,* edited by Richard S. Kirkendall. Columbia: University of Missouri Press, 1967, pp. 187–212.

Bernstein, Barton J. "America in War and Peace: The Test of Liberalism." In *Towards a New Past: Dissenting Essays in American History,* edited by Barton J. Bernstein. New York: Pantheon Books, 1968, pp. 289–321.

————. "American Foreign Policy and the Origins of the Cold War." In *Politics and Policies of the Truman Administration,* edited by Barton J. Bernstein. Chicago: Quadrangle Books, 1970, pp. 15–77.

———. "The Ambiguous Legacy: The Truman Administration and Civil Rights." In *Politics and Policies of the Truman Administration,* edited by Barton J. Bernstein. Chicago: Quadrangle Books, 1970, pp. 269–314.

———. "The Postwar Famine and Price Control, 1946," *Agricultural History* 38 (October 1964): 235–240.

———. "The Removal of War Production Board Controls of Business, 1944–1947." *Business History Review* 39 (Summer 1965): 243–260.

———. "The Truman Administration and Its Reconversion Wage Policy." *Labor History* 6 (Fall 1965): 214–231.

———. "The Truman Administration and the Steel Strike of 1946." *Journal of American History* 52 (March 1966): 791–803.

Bickerton, Ian J. "President Truman's Recognition of Israel." *American Jewish History Quarterly* 58 (December 1968): 173–240.

Budenz, Louis. "How the Reds Snatched Away Henry Wallace." *Colliers* 122 (September 18, 1948): 14–15, 76–77.

Davies, Richard O. "Social Welfare Policies." In *The Truman Period as a Research Field,* edited by Richard Kirkendall. Columbia: University of Missouri Press, 1967, pp. 149–186.

———. "Whistle-Stopping Through Ohio." *Ohio History* 71 (July 1962): 113–123.

Divine, Robert A. "The Cold War and the Election of 1948," *Journal of American History* 59 (June 1972): 90–110.

DuBois, W. E. B. "From McKinley to Wallace." *Masses & Mainstream* 1 (August 1948): 3–13.

Garson, Robert A. "The Alienation of the South: A Crisis for Harry S. Truman and the Democratic Party, 1945–1948." *Missouri Historical Review* 64 (July 1970): 448–471.

Hale, William Harlan. "What Makes Wallace Run?" *Harper's* 196 (March 1948): 241–248.

Hamby, Alonzo L. "Henry A. Wallace, the Liberals, and Soviet-American Relations." *Review of Politics* 30 (April 1968): 153–169.

———. "Sixty Million Jobs and the People's Revolution: The Liberals, The New Deal and World War II." *Historian* 30 (August 1968): 578–598.

———. "The Liberals, Truman, and FDR as Symbol and Myth." *Journal of American History* 56 (March 1970): 859–867.

———. "The Vital Center, The Fair Deal, and the Quest for a Liberal Political Economy." *American Historical Review* 77 (June 1972): 653–678.

Havemann, Ernest. "Clark Clifford," *Life* 22 (January 27, 1947): 45–46, 48, 51, 53.

Humphrey, Hubert. "A Reply to Rex Tugwell." *Progressive* 12 (April 1949): 7–9.

Jackson, Gardner. "Henry Wallace; A Divided Mind." *Atlantic Monthly* 182 (August 1948): 27–33.

Kirkendall, Richard S. "Election of 1948." In *History of American Presidential Elections,* IV, edited by Arthur M. Schlesinger, Jr. New York: Chelsea House Publishers, 1971, pp. 3099–3211.

———. "Harry Truman." In *America's Eleven Greatest Presidents,* edited by Morton Borden. Chicago: Rand McNally, 1971, pp. 255–288.

Kirschner, Don A. "Henry A. Wallace as Farm Editor." *American Quarterly* 17 (Summer 1965): 187–202.

Lee R. Alton. "The Truman 80th Congress Struggle Over Tax Policy." *Historian* 33 (November 1970): 68–82.

———. "The Turnip Session of the Do-Nothing Congress: Presidential Campaign Strategy." *Southwestern Social Science Quarterly* 44 (Summer 1967): 1–21.

Leeds, Morton. "The AFL in the 1948 Elections." *Social Research* 30 (December 1951): 162–171.

McCoy, Donald R., and Ruetten, Richard T. "The Civil Rights Movement, 1949–1954." *Midwest Quarterly* 11 (Autumn 1969): 11–34.

Neustadt, Richard E. "Congress and the Fair Deal: A Legislative Balance Sheet." In *The Shaping of Twentieth Century America: Interpretive Articles,* edited by Richard M. Abrams and Lawrence W. Levine, Boston: Little, Brown, 1965.

Peterson, F. Ross. "Fighting the Drive Toward War: Glen H. Taylor, the 1948 Progressives, and the Draft." *Pacific Northwest Quarterly* (January 1970): 41–45.

———. "Harry S. Truman and His Critics: The 1948 Progressives and the Origins of the Cold War." In *Essays on Radicalism in Contemporary America,* edited by Leon Borden Blair. Austin: University of Texas Press, 1972, pp. 32–62.

———. "Protest Songs for Peace and Freedom: People's Songs and the 1948 Progressives." *Rocky Mountain Social Sciences Journal* 9 (January 1972): 1–10.

Powers, Richard J. "Who Fathered Containment?" *International Studies Quarterly* 15 (December 1971): 526–543.

Pratt, William C. "Glen H. Taylor: Public Image and Reality." *Pacific Northwest Quarterly* 60 (January 1969): 10–16.

———. Senator Glen H. Taylor: Questioning American Unilateralism." In *Cold War Critics,* edited by Thomas G. Paterson. Chicago: Quadrangle Books, 1971, pp. 140–166.

Radosh, Ronald, and Liggio, Leonard. "Henry A. Wallace and the Open Door." In *Cold War Critics,* edited by Thomas G. Paterson. Chicago: Quadrangle Books, 1972, pp. 76–113.

Sander, Alfred D. "Truman and the National Security Council: 1945–1947." *Journal of American History* 59 (September 1972): 369–388.

Schapsmeier, Edward L., and Schapsmeier, Frederick H. "A Prophet in Politics: The Public Career of Henry A. Wallace." *Annals of Iowa* 39 (Summer 1967): 1–21.

———. "Henry A. Wallace: Agrarian Idealist or Agricultural Realist." *Agricultural History* 41 (April 1967): 127–137.

———. "Henry A. Wallace: New Deal Philospher," *Historian* 22 (February 1970): 177–190.

Shogan, Robert. "1948 Election." *American Heritage* 19 (June 1968): 22–31, 104–111.

Sitkoff, Harvard. "Harry Truman and the Election of 1948: The Coming of Age of Civil Rights in American Politics." *Journal of Southern History* 37 (November 1971): 597–616.

Stebbins, Philip E. "Truman and the Seizure of Steel: a Failure in Communication." *Historian* 34 (November 1971): 1–21.

Straight, Michael. "Days with Henry Wallace." *New Republic* 153 (December 4, 1965): 9–11.

Theoharis, Athan. "The Escalation of the Loyalty Program." In *Politics and Policies of the Truman Administration,* edited by Barton J. Bernstein. Chicago: Quadrangle Books, 1970, pp. 242–268.

———. "The Rhetoric of Politics: Foreign Policy, Internal Security, and Domestic Politics in the Truman Era, 1945–1950." In *Politics and Policies of the Truman Administration,* edited by Barton J. Bernstein. Chicago: Quadrangle Books, 1970, 196–241.

———. "The Truman Presidency; Trial and Error." *Wisconsin Magazine of History* 55 (August 1971): 49–58.

Tugwell, Rexford Guy. "Progressives and the Presidency." *Progressive* 13 (April 1949): 5–7.

VanAuken, Cecilia. "The Negro Press in the 1948 Election." *Journalism Quarterly* 26 (December 1949): 431–435.

Vaughan, Philip. "President Truman's Committee on Civil Rights: The Urban Implications." *Missouri Historical Review* 66 (April 1972): 413–430.

Wallace, Henry A. "Henry Wallace Tells of his Political Odyssey." *Life* 40 (May 14, 1956): 174-190.

———. "I Shall Run in 1948." *Vital Speeches* 14 January 1, 1948): 172-174.

———. "The Path to Peace with Russia." *New Republic* 115 (September 30, 1946): 401–403.

———. "The Way to Peace." *Vital Speeches* 12 (October 1, 1946): 738–741.

———. "Why a Third Party in 1948?" *Annals of the American Academy of Political and Social Science* 259 (September, 1948): 10–16.

White, Leigh. "Truman's One-Man Brain Trust." *Saturday Evening Post* 220 (October 4, 1947): 30–31, 106, 108, 113.

Wyatt, Wilson. "Creed for Liberals: A Ten Point Program." *New York Times Magazine* (July 27, 1947): 7, 35–37.

Yarnell, Allen. "The Democratic Party's Response to the Progressive Party in 1948." *Research Studies* 39 (March 1971): 20–32.

———. "Liberals in Action: The ADA, Henry Wallace and the 1948 Presidential Election," *Research Studies* 40 (December 1972): 260–273.

———. "Pension Politics in Washington State, 1948." *Pacific Northwest Quarterly* 61 (July 1970): 147–155.

B. Books

Abels, Jules. *Out of the Jaws of Victory*. New York: Henry Holt, 1959.

Abrams, Richard M., and Levine, Lawrence W., eds. *The Shaping of Twentieth Century America: Interpretive Articles*. Boston: Little, Brown, 1965.

Acheson, Dean. *Present at the Creation*. New York: Norton, 1969.

Allen, Robert S., and Shannon, William V. *The Truman Merry-Go-Round*. New York: Vanguard Press, 1950.

Anderson, Patrick. *The President's Men*. Garden City: Doubleday, 1968.

Anson, Robert Sam. *McGovern: A Biography*. New York: Holt, Rinehart and Winston, 1972.

Aronson, James. *The Press and the Cold War*. Indianapolis: Bobbs-Merrill, 1970.

Barkley, Alben W. *That Reminds Me*. Garden City: Doubleday, 1954.

Berelson, Bernard R.; Lazarfield, Paul F.; and McPhee, William N. *Voting*. Chicago: University of Chicago Press, 1954.

Berman, William C. *The Politics of Civil Rights in the Truman Admnistration*. Columbus: Ohio State University Press, 1970.

Bernstein, Barton J., ed. *Politics and Policies of the Truman Administration*. Chicago: Quadrangle Books, 1970

———. *Towards a New Past: Dissenting Essays in American History*. New York: Pantheon Books, 1968.

———. and Matusow, Allen J., eds. *The Truman Administration: A Documentary History*. New York: Harper & Row, 1966.

Bliven, Bruce. *Five Million Words: An Autobiography*. New York: John Day Company, 1970.

Bowles, Chester. *Promises to Keep: My Years in Public Life, 1941–1969*. New York: Harper & Row, 1971.

Brock, Clifton. *Americans for Democratic Action: Its Role in National Politics*. Washington, D.C.: Public Affairs Press, 1962.

Byrnes, James F. *All in One Lifetime*. New York: Harper and Brothers, 1958.

————. *Speaking Frankly*. New York: Harper and Brothers, 1947.

Campbell, Agnus; Converse, Philip E.; Miller, Warren E.; and Stokes, Donald E. *The American Voter; An Abridgement*. New York: John Wiley, 1964.

Carr, Albert Z. *Truman, Stalin and Peace*. Garden City: Doubleday, 1950.

Cochran, Bert. *Harry Truman and the Crisis Presidency*. New York: Funk & Wagnalls, 1973.

Coffin, Tris. *Missouri Compromise*. Boston: Little, Brown, 1947.

Coit, Margaret. *Mr. Baruch*. Boston: Houghton Mifflin, 1957.

Curry, George. *James F. Byrnes*. New York: Cooper Square Publishers, 1965.

Dalfiume, Richard S. *Desegregation of the U.S. Armed Forces: Fighting on Two Fronts, 1939–1953*. Columbia: University of Missouri Press, 1969.

Daniels, Jonathan. *The Man of Independence*. Philadelphia: J. B. Lippincott, 1950.

Davidson, Jo. *Between Sittings: An Informal Autobiography of Jo Davidson*. New York: Dial Press, 1951.

Davies, Richard O. *Housing Reform During the Truman Administration*. Columbia: University of Missouri Press, 1966.

DeCaux, Len. *Labor Radical*. Boston: Beacon Press, 1970.

Dorsett, Lyle W. *The Pendergast Machine*. New York: Oxford University Press, 1968.

Douglas, Paul H. *In the Fullness of Time: The Memoirs of Paul H. Douglas*. New York: Harcourt, Brace Jovanovich, 1972.

Druks, Herbert. *Harry S. Truman and the Russians, 1945–1953*. New York: Robert Speller & Sons, 1966.

Farrar, Ronald T. *Reluctant Servant: The Story of Charles G. Ross*. Columbia: University of Missouri Press, 1969.

Feis, Herbert. *From Trust to Terror: The Onset of the Cold War, 1945–1950*. New York: W. W. Norton, 1970.

Ferrell, Robert H. *George C. Marshall*. New York: Cooper Square Publishers, 1966.

Freeland, Richard M. *The Truman Doctrine and the Origins of McCarthyism: Foreign Policy, Domestic Politics, and Internal Security, 1946–1948*. New York: Alfred A. Knopf, 1972.

Gaddis, John Lewis. *The United States and the Origins of the Cold War, 1941–1947*. New York: Columbia University Press, 1972.

Gardner, Lloyd C. *Architects of Illusion: Men and Ideas in American Foreign Policy, 1941–1949*. Chicago: Quadrangle Books, 1970.

Gerson, Louis L. *The Hyphenate in Recent American Politics and Diplomacy*. Lawrence: University of Kansas Press, 1964.

Bibliography   *145*

Goldman, Eric F. *The Crucial Decade and After*. New York: Vintage Books, 1960.
————. *Rendezvous with Destiny*. New York: Vintage Books, 1956.
Griffith, Robert. *The Politics of Fear: Joseph R. McCarthy and the Senate*. Lexington: University of Kentucky Press, 1970.
Hammond, Paul Y. *The Cold War Years: American Foreign Policy Since 1945*. New York: Harcourt, Brace & World, 1969.
Hareven, Tamara. *Eleanor Roosevelt: An American Conscience*. Chicago: Quadrangle Books, 1968.
Harper, Alan D. *The Politics of Loyalty: The White House and the Communist Issue, 1946–1952*. Westport, Conn.: Greenwood Publishing, 1969.
Hartmann, Susan M. *Truman and the 80th Congress*. Columbia: University of Missouri Press, 1971.
Helm, William P. *Harry Truman: A Political Biography*. New York: Duell, Sloan & Pearce, 1947.
Hesseltine, William B. *The Rise and Fall of Third Parties*. Washington, D.C.: Public Affairs Press, 1948.
Hillman, William. *Mr. President*. New York: Farrar, Straus and Young, 1952.
Howe, Irving, and Coser, Lewis. *The American Communist Party*. Boston: Beacon Press, 1957.
Huthmacher, J. Joseph. *Senator Robert F. Wagner and the Rise of Urban Liberalism*. New York: Atheneum Books, 1968.
Johnpoll, Bernard K. *Pacifist's Progress: Norman Thomas and the Decline of American Socialism*. Chicago: Quadrangle Books, 1970.
Johnson, Walter. *1600 Pennsylvania Avenue*. Boston: Little, Brown, 1963.
Kennan, George F. *Memoirs, 1925–1950*. Boston: Little, Brown, 1967.
Kingdon, Frank. *An Uncommon Man: Henry Wallace and Sixty Million Jobs*. New York: Readers Press, 1945.
Kirkendall, Richard S., ed. *The Truman Period as a Research Field*. Columbia: University of Missouri Press, 1967.
Kolko, Joyce, and Kolko, Gabriel. *The Limits of Power: The World and United States Foreign Policy, 1945–1954*. New York: Harper & Row, 1972.
Krock, Arthur. *Memoirs: Sixty Years on the Firing Line*. New York: Funk & Wagnalls, 1968.
LaFeber, Walter. *America, Russia, and the Cold War, 1945–1971*. New York: John Wiley, 1972.
Lash, Joseph P. *Eleanor: The Years Alone*. New York: W. W. Norton, 1972.
Latham, Earl. *The Communist Controversy in Washington: From the*

New Deal to McCarthy. Cambridge: Harvard University Press, 1966.

Lee, R. Alton. *Truman and Taft-Hartley: A Question of Mandate*. Lexington: University of Kentucky Press, 1966.

Lord, Russell. *The Wallaces of Iowa*. Boston: Houghton Mifflin, 1947.

Lubell, Samuel. *The Future of American Politics*, 3rd ed. rev. New York: Harper & Row, 1965.

McClure, Arthur F. *The Truman Administration and the Problems of Postwar Labor, 1945–1948*. Rutherford, N.J.: Farleigh Dickinson University Press, 1969.

MacDonald, Dwight. *Henry Wallace: The Man and the Myth*. New York: Vanguard Press, 1948.

MacDougall, Curtis D. *Gideon's Army*. 3 vols. New York: Marzani & Munsell, 1965.

McGrath, J. Howard. *The Power of the People*. New York: John Messner, 1948.

McNaughton, Frank, and Hehmeyer, Walter. *Harry Truman: President*. New York: McGraw-Hill, 1948.

Markowitz, Norman D. *The Rise and Fall of the People's Century: Henry A. Wallace and American Liberalism, 1941–1948*. New York: Free Press, 1973.

Matusow, Allen J. *Farm Policies and Politics in the Truman Years*. Cambridge: Harvard University Press, 1967.

Millis, Walter, ed. *The Forrestal Diaries*. New York: Viking Press, 1951.

Moon, Henry Lee. *Balance of Power: The Negro Vote*. Garden City: Doubleday, 1948.

Mosteller, Frederick, et al. *The Pre-Election Polls of 1948*. New York: Social Science Research Council, 1949.

Paterson, Thomas G., ed. *Cold War Critics*. Chicago: Quadrangle Books, 1971.

Phillips, Cabell. *The Truman Presidency: The History of a Triumphant Succession*. New York: Macmillan, 1966.

Porter, Kirk H., and Johnson, Donald Bruce, compilers. *National Party Platforms, 1840–1964*. Urbana: University of Illinois Press, 1966.

Public Papers of the Presidents of the United States. Harry S. Truman. 9 vols. Washington, D.C.: Government Printing Office, 1961–1966.

Record, Wilson. *The Negro and the Communist Party*. Chapel Hill: University of North Carolina Press, 1951.

Redding, Jack. *Inside the Democratic Party*. Indianapolis: Bobbs-Merrill, 1958.

Rogow, Arnold. *James Forrestal: A Study of Personality, Politics, and Policy*. New York: Macmillan, 1963.

Rosenboom, Eugene H. *A Short History of Presidential Elections*. New York: Collier Books, 1967.

Ross, Irwin. *The Loneliest Campaign: The Truman Victory of 1948.* New York: New American Library, 1968.

Sawyer, Charles. *Concerns of a Conservative Democrat.* Carbondale: Southern Illinois University Press, 1968.

Scammon, Richard M., ed. *American at the Polls.* Pittsburgh: University Press, 1965.

Schaffer, Alan. *Vito Marcantonio, Radical in Congress.* Syracuse: Syracuse University Press, 1966.

Schapsmeier, Edward L., and Schapsmeier, Frederick H. *Henry A. Wallace of Iowa: The Agrarian Years.* Ames: Iowa State University Press, 1968.

————. *Prophet in Politics: Henry A. Wallace and the War Years, 1940–1965.* Ames: Iowa State University Press, 1970.

Schlesinger, Arthur M., Jr., ed. *History of American Presidential Elections, IV.* New York: Chelsea House, 1971.

————. *The Vital Center: The Politics of Freedom.* Boston: Houghton Mifflin, 1949.

Schmidt, Karl M. *Henry A. Wallace: Quixotic Crusade, 1948.* Syracuse: Syracuse University Press, 1960.

Seidler, Murray B. *Norman Thomas: Respectable Rebel.* Syracuse: Syracuse University Press, 1961.

Shannon, David A. *The Decline of American Communism.* New York: Harcourt, Brace, 1959.

Shields, James M. *Mr. Progressive: A Biography of Elmer A. Benson.* Minneapolis: T. S. Denison, 1971.

Starobin, Joseph R. *American Communism in Crisis, 1943–1957.* Cambridge: Harvard University Press, 1972.

Steinberg, Alfred. *The Man From Missouri: The Life and Times of Harry S. Truman.* New York: G. P. Putman's Sons, 1962.

Stone, I. F. *The Truman Era.* New York: Monthly Review Press, 1953.

Theoharis, Athan. *Seeds of Repression: Harry S. Truman and the Origins of McCarthyism.* Chicago: Quadrangle Books, 1971.

Truman, Harry S. *Memoirs.* 2 vols. Garden City: Doubleday, 1955–1956.

Truman, Margaret. *Harry S. Truman.* New York: William Morrow, 1973.

Tugwell, Rexford G. *A Chronicle of Jeopardy—1945–1955.* Chicago: University of Chicago Press, 1955.

————. *Off Course: From Truman to Nixon.* New York: Praiger Publishers, 1971.

Ulam, Adam B. *The Rivals: America and Russia Since World War II.* New York: Viking Press, 1971.

Vandenberg, Arthur H., Jr. *The Private Papers of Senator Vandenberg.* Boston: Houghton Mifflin, 1952.

Wallace, Henry A. *The Century of the Common Man.* Edited by Russell Lord. New York: Reynal & Hitchcock, 1943.

———. *The Price of Free World Victory.* New York: L. B. Fisher, 1942.

———. *Sixty Million Jobs.* New York: Reynal & Hitchcock, 1945.

———. *Toward World Peace.* New York: Reynal & Hitchcock, 1948.

——— and Steiger, Andrew J. *Soviet Asia Mission.* New York: Reynal & Hitchcock, 1946.

Wittner, Lawrence S. *Rebels Against War. The American Peace Movement, 1941–1960.* New York: Columbia University Press, 1969.

Wechsler, James A. *The Age of Suspicion.* New York: Random House, 1953.

C. Newspapers and Periodicals

ADA World	*Washington Post*	*Progressive*
New York Star	*Crisis*	*Public Opinion Quarterly*
New York Times	*Nation*	*Time*
PM	*New Republic*	

Note: After the completion of this manuscript, *The Price of Vision: The Diary of Henry A. Wallace, 1942–1946,* edited by John Morton Blum (Boston: Houghton Mifflin, 1973), was published. The material contained in the diary does not contradict the interpretation presented in this book but does add much to an understanding of Wallace's personal view of Harry Truman and matters in general. For more Wallace material, scholars must await the opening of the Henry Agard Wallace Oral History Interview housed in the Columbia University Oral History collection. The Interview is scheduled to be opened in 1975.

INDEX

Abels, Jules, xi
Acheson, Dean, 104
ADA. *See* Americans for Democratic Action
ADA World, 90, 93
Aircraft industry: Wallace favors government ownership, 65
Alexander, Raymond Pace, 73
Alfange, Dean, 52, 57
Allen, Robert S., 21
Amalgamated Clothing Workers, 53
American Labor party: support for Wallace, 19; Isacson victory, 52–57; influence on Democrats, 62
Americans for Democratic Action: opposition to Wallace and Progressives, 40, 46, 90, 93–94, 96–103, 106–107; Tyler memo to, on Isacson, 56; founding and makeup of, 88–89; anti-Communism of, 89, 97, 102, 107; definition of liberalism, 91–92; Tugwell opposes, 94–95; Humphrey defends, 95; Wallace a threat to, 97; possible anti-Wallace agreement with Democrats, 97–98, 132 n. 37; Wallaceites ignore attacks of, 102; opposed Truman, 132 n. 35
American Society of Newspaper Editors, 19
American Veterans Committee, 12, 93
Anderson, Patrick, 36
Anson, Robert Sam, 133 n. 61
Anti-Communism: in Clifford's strategy, 33, 36, 37; and Catholic vote, 36, 109; Progressives oppose discrimination based on, 68; development of, 77, 114; Truman's use of, 77, 79, 109; in California, 82; of ADA, 88, 89, 92, 94, 97, 102, 107. *See also* Communists
Atlanta Constitution: reaction to Wallace candidacy, 48–49
Atomic bomb: Truman's use of, 1; Wallace on use of, 4, 6–7

Baldwin, C. B. (Beanie), x, 6, 26, 27, 31, 35
Baltimore Sun: on Truman attitude toward Wallace, 19
Barkley, Alben, 105
Barriere, John, 113–114
Batt, William L., Jr., 72–74, 78, 82, 83, 85, 98
Belair, Felix, Jr., 18
Bell, David, 83
Berle, A. A.: opposes Wallace, 57, 105
Berlin blockade, xii, 63, 76–77
Berman, William, 71
Bernstein, Barton, 3, 71
Birkhead, Kenneth M., 74–75, 78, 98
Black vote: Clifford strategy memo on, 34–35, 44; fears of defection to GOP, 52, 72, 73; impact of Wallace candidacy on, 52, 71, 74, 75; Democrats try to keep, 68–69, 71–73, 75, 85; and civil rights gains, 86; Wallace strength in New York City, 128 n. 49
Blaine, Anita McCormick, 112, 129 n. 74
Bowles, Chester, 55, 83
Boykin, Frank, 20
Britain. *See* Great Britain
Brock, Clifton, 106
Brotherhood of Railway Trainmen, 23
Brown, Clarence, 49
Brown, Edmund G., 46
Bruce, Donald, 13
Burnham, James, 90
Byrnes, James, 7, 10

California: Wallace chances in, 52; Truman's speech in Los Angeles, 81–82; Democrats' situation in, 82–83
California Democratic State Central Comittee, 26
Camacho, Manuel, 3

Campbell, Angus, 108
Capital Comment: McGrath on Wallace in, 50–51
Carr, Albert, 83, 130 n. 86
Carter, John Franklin, 84
Catholic vote, 36, 109
Chapman, Oscar, 36
Chicago: McNaughton fears Wallace will damage Truman in, 52
China: Wallace criticizes policy toward, 59, 67
Churchill, Winston: "Iron Curtain" speech, 3–4
CIO, 130 n. 1
Civil rights: events during 1948 on, 35; some feel Wallace influenced, 35, 71; Wallace on, 66, 126 n. 10; Truman speeches on, 68–69, 72, 73, 75; some feel strong plank on thrust on Truman, 74, 128 n. 61; gains in, 86; ADA critical of Wallace policy on, 101; Elsey on handling of, 127 n. 45
Clemens, Cyril, 15
Clifford, Clark, xi, 22, 58, 82, 83; favors Taft-Hartley veto, 24; background of, 28–29; strategy memo, 28–45, 74; Truman follows advice of on Wallace, 49; on black vote, 52, 73, 75; Truman follows advice of on State of the Union message, 68, 70–71; advice of on acceptance speech, 79; guidelines on Truman image, 85–86, 114; on ADA, 98
Cold war: Wallace on, 2, 64, 90, 104, 109, 113; tied to domestic politics, 37; Clifford recommends use of in strategy, 42; Freeland on, 77; as problem for liberals, 87, 88; and ADA, 107; rejection of by Progressive party, 111
Communists: Democrats link with Wallace, 31, 32, 50–61, 60–61; in Clifford strategy against Wallace, 32–33, 39; strength seen in Isacson victory, 54–56; Truman charges third party connected with, 58, 60–61, 81, 83–85; Wallace answers charges of link with, 59, 65; effect of on Progressive party strength, 63, 84, 110; in California, 82; as problem for liberals, 87, 88, 89; ADA rejects, 89, 90, 92, 94; ADA

uses issue of against Wallace, 92–107; in Progressive party, 104; Democrats' hard line on, 111; Wallace on, 113
Congress: Clifford suggests use of in strategy, 38, 42; Truman use of as issue, 63, 71, 85
Connally, Thomas: critical of Wallace, 10
Connecticut: McNaughton predicts Wallace strength in, 52
Connelly, Matthew, 46, 83, 130 n. 86
Conservation: as issue, in Clifford's memo, 43
Converse, Philip, 108
Cost of living issue, 37
Coughlin, Father, 109
Crisis: on Wallace's civil rights record, 101
Czechoslovakia: role of Russian takeover in Wallace campaign, 58–59, 63, 76, 99

Daniels, Josephus, 16
Davidson, C. Girard, 28
Davies, Richard O., 43, 71
DeCaux, Len, x
Democratic National Committee, 22–23, 38
Democratic party: opinions on Progressive influence on, x–xii, 62, 86, 111, 113, 114; early Wallace criticism of, 15; and labor, 23–24; liberal element wins out in, 28; Clifford strategy memo on, 28–45; reaction to Wallace candidacy, 49–52, 56; and Isacson victory, 53–57, 61; Progressives attack, 65–66; response to Progressive position, 68–75, 80, 84; civil rights plank, 75–76; foreign policy, 79–80; in California, 82; Wallace supports some candidates of, 83; image of, 85; and ADA, 97–98
Democrats for Wallace, 118 n. 1
DeNigris, Joseph, 52
Dennis, Eugene, 99
Dewey, Thomas E., 30, 34, 44, 85
Dixiecrats, 108
Domestic issues: opinions on Progressive influence on, xii, 62; Wallace on, 2, 64, 126 n. 10; in Clifford strategy, 37; linked to foreign

policy, 42; and Republican influence on Democrats' program, 62; and Progressive program, 68; Truman policies on, 68–70, 114; ADA position on, 91; Tugwell critical of ADA stand on, 95; ADA attacks Wallace on, 101; Progressives did not influence Democrats on, 110, 111
Douglas, Helen Gahagan, 27, 82, 83
Douglas, William, O., 96
Draft. *See* Selective service
Dubinsky, David, 132 n. 36

Education: Truman proposals for government aid, 69
Einstein, Albert: praises Wallace, 12
Eisenhower, Dwight David, 96
Elsey, George M., 8, 22, 29, 58, 80, 127 nn. 32, 45
European Recovery Program. *See* Marshall Plan
Ewing, Oscar, 28

Fair Employment Practices Committee, 35, 44, 73
Farm policy: Wallace on, 66; Truman's, 70
Farm vote: in Clifford's strategy, 33
Field, Frederick V., 101
Flynn, Edward, 54, 55, 56, 57
Folliard, Edward, 48–49
Foreign policy: Progressive party position on, ix, 27, 67–68, 91; effect of Progressive party on, xii, 37, 62–63, 86, 109–110, 113–114; Truman's, 1, 9, 79; Wallace's dissatisfaction with, 2–5; Wallace speaks on, 5–8, 10, 11, 13, 17, 54, 64, 66, 90; Truman defends, 21, 70; in Clifford memo, 31, 36–37, 41–42; tied to domestic politics, 37; Truman keeps out of campaign, 63, 76; and Russian actions, 77; and liberalism, 87; ADA on, 90, 100, 105; Tugwell criticizes ADA on, 95; McGovern supports Wallace on, 104; Wallace's views change on, 113
Forrestal, James, 20
Fortas, Abe, 105
Foster, William Z., 99
Freeland, Richard M., 77

Friendly Sons of St. Patrick: Truman addresses, 57–58

Gallup poll: on Wallace vote, 126 n. 67
Germany: Wallace criticizes Marshall plan for rebuilding, 66, 67
Gideon's Army, 84
Great Britain: Wallace critical of foreign policy of, 6, 93, 99, 100
Greece: U.S. aid to, 17; Wallace criticizes policy toward, 59, 67
Griffith, Robert, 107

Halleck, Charles: on Wallace candidacy, 49
Hamby, Alonzo, 53
Hammond, Paul, 63
Hannegan, Robert, 24
Harper, Alan, 84
Health care: Truman proposal for, 69
Henderson, Leon, 90, 94–95, 103, 132 n. 37; and anti-Wallace pamphlet, 98–101
Hesseltine, William B., ix, x
Hicks, John D., ix
Hippelheuser, Richard, 4
Hiss, Alger, case, 83
Hoeber, Johannes, 97–98
Holifield, Chet, 82
Hoover, Herbert, 40
Housing: as issue, 37, 43, 63, 69
Humphrey, Hubert, 95, 96, 107, 113

Ickes, Harold, 66, 104
Independent Citizens Committee of the Arts, Sciences and Professions, 5, 89
Inflation: E. Roosevelt on, 54; Wallace on, 66; Truman on, 70
International Ladies' Garment Workers' Union, 56
Isaacs, Stanley, 88
Isacson, Leo: victory of, 52–57, 60–61
Israel: Truman's recognition of, 36
Italian vote, 36
Italy: ADA attacks Wallace position on, 101

Jewish vote: in Clifford's strategy, 35–36; effects of in Isacson victory, 53

Kenny, Robert W., 14–15, 118 n. 1
Keyserling, Leon, 28
Kingdon, Frank, 99
Kirchway, Freda, 47
Kirkendall, Richard S., xii, 63
Korean War: and Wallace's break with Progressives, 112
Krock, Arthur, 20

Labor: keeping in Democratic coalition, 23–25, 34, 38–39, 85; Wallace calls Truman hostile to, 66; ADA critical of Wallace policy toward, 101
LaFeber, Walter, xi–xii, 63
La Follette, Robert, Jr., 40
La Follette, Robert, Sr., x, 67
Lawrence, David, 48
Lee, R. Alton, 24
Lerner, Max, 12–13; on Wallace candidacy, 47; on Isacson victory, 55
Liberal party: and Isacson victory, 52–54, 56; attacks Wallace, 57
Liberals: 87–107; strength of in Democratic party, 28; mentioned in Clifford strategy memo, 34, 39–40; Truman image as, 40, 61, 85–86; effect of Wallace candidacy on, 46, 47; Democrats risk losing, 59; and civil rights plank, 71; Wallace appeals for support of, 81; in California, 82; and cold war, 87, 88; ADA as voice of, 88, 107; defined by Wallace, 90–91; ADA definition of, 91–92; Wyatt fears third party will hurt, 92–93; ADA identifies with anti-Communism, 94, 97; ADA attack on with "Appeal to Liberals," 104–105; and red-baiting, 114
Life magazine: Wallace in, 8; on Clifford, 29; Burnham article in, 90
Loeb, James, Jr., 88–89, 93–94, 95–96, 97, 98, 102, 103, 104–105
Los Angeles: Truman speech at, 81–83
Lubell, Samuel, 109
Lucas, Scott, 50

McCarthyism, 33, 85, 107
McCormack, John: on Wallace candidacy, 50; on Isacson victory, 55

MacDougall, Curtis, xi, 25, 48, 106, 113
McGill, Ralph: view of Wallace candidacy, 48
McGovern, George: supports Wallace, 104, 133 n. 61
McGrath, J. Howard, 26, 78, 132 n. 37; on Wallace, 50–51, 60; on Isacson election, 54, 56
McNaughton, Frank: appraisal of Wallace impact, 51–52, 60
Madison Square Garden: Wallace speech at, 5–10, 100
Marshall, George C., 37, 41
Marshall Plan, 14, 25, 41; Wallace opposes, 25; and farm vote, 33; Truman pushes, 58, 77; Progressives attack, 67; ADA supports, 91
Martin, Joseph, 51
Masaryk, Jan, 76
Middle West: Wallace chances in, 52; Truman's Communism speech in, 83
Miller, Warren, 108
Minimum wage, as campaign issue, 63, 70
Minorities: in Clifford's strategy plan, 34–36, 44. *See also* Black vote; Catholic vote; Jewish vote
Mitchell, Hugh, 128 n. 61
Mobile Register: reaction to Wallace candidacy, 48
Montgomery Advertiser, reaction to Wallace candidacy, 48
Morse, David, 28
Moscow, Warren: on Isacson victory, 55
Murphy, Charles S., 28, 82, 83, 84, 127 n. 32, 130 n. 86
Murphy, Franklin, 12
Murray, Philip, 130 n. 1
Myers, Frank, 73

Nashville Tennessean: reaction to candidacy, 48
Nation: on Wallace candidacy, 46, 47
National Citizens Political Action Committee (NCPAC), 5–6, 89
Negro Digest: supports Wallace, 12
Negro vote. *See* Black vote
New Deal: Democrats and Progressives vie for support of, xi, 1, 18, 23, 25, 66, 85, 100; and ADA mem-

bership, 88; effect of on Wallace campaign, 95

New Masses, 101

New Republic: Wallace as editor, 2, 11–12, 13, 16; Loeb-Isaacs arguments in, 88–89

New York City: Isacson victory in, 52–57, 60–61; black vote in, 72–73, 128 n. 49; civil rights speech in Harlem, 75

New York Herald Tribune: reaction to Wallace candidacy, 48; on Isacson victory, 52–53

New York Mirror: reaction to Wallace candidacy, 48

New York Post: anti-Wallace material requested from, 96; Kingdon in, on Wallace candidacy, 99

New York Star: on Truman victory, 111

New York Times: reaction to Wallace candidacy, 47; on Isacson victory, 55; denunciation of Wallace, 78; on Truman victory, 111

New York Times Magazine: Wyatt's "Creed for Liberals" in, 91

Niebuhr, Reinhold, 104

Norris, George, x

Oklahoma City: Truman speech at, 83–84

O'Konski, Alvin E., 90

Palestine issue: importance in Isacson victory, 54, 56

Pauley, Edwin, 121 n. 44

PCA. *See* Progressive Citizens of America

Peace issue: Wallace on, 2, 4–6, 11, 58–59, 64, 93, 109, 113; Progressive party focus on, 67–68; in Truman campaign, 85

Pepper, Claude, 15, 18, 62, 112, 118 n. 2

Peterson, Frank Ross, 116 n. 17, 126 n. 2

Phillips, Cabell, 29

PM: on Wallace candidacy, 47; on Isacson victory, 55

Potsdam Conference, 29

President's Committee on Civil Rights, 68, 72, 75

Pressure groups: in Clifford strategy memo, 33–36

Price controls, 37

Prices, high: as campaign issue, 37, 43, 63

Progressive Citizens of America, 15, 27, 89, 90, 99

Progressive magazine, x, 95

Progressive party: aims, ix; opinions on impact of, x–xii, 62–63, 74–76, 79, 111,; ADA fight against, 40, 88, 93, 98–101, 105, 107; high point of campaign of, 52; reasons for formation of, 65, 113; attack on Democrats, 65–66; attacks Truman, 66; platform, 67–68; link to Roosevelt, 67; Democrats' response to, 67–71, 78–79, 80, 84; influenced Vinson mission, 80; did not influence Democratic policies, 80, 109–111, 113, 114; Truman speeches on, 80–85; supports some Democrats, 83; some members of return to Democratic party, 84; Norman Thomas attacks, 87; defines a liberal, 90–91; Tugwell on, 95, 110; ignores ADA attacks, 102; Loeb attacks, 102–103; Whitney opposes, 103; Communists in, 104, 113; in election, 108; Wallace resigns from, 112; as scapegoat, 114

Progressives of 1912 and 1924, x

Propper, Karl, 52

Racial discrimination: Progressives' and Democrats' programs on, 68; Truman on, 73. *See also* Civil rights

Raleigh News and Observer: reaction to Wallace in, 48, 49

Rauh, Joseph, 98, 104

Rayburn, Sam, 60

Redding, Jack, 78

Republican party: and civil rights, 35, 72–73, 76; opinions on impact of Wallace candidacy, 46, 47, 49; reaction to Wallace candidacy, 49, 51; and black vote, 52, 72, 73; influence on Democratic domestic program, 62, 76; Truman on, 81, 84

Reuther, Walter, 132 n. 36

Roosevelt, Eleanor: on Isacson victory and Wallace impact, 54–55; on ADA, 89

Roosevelt, Franklin Delano: Truman tries to carry out policies of, 1; Wallace identifies his policies with, 64, 106; Progressives try to link with, 65, 66–67, 68; ADA denies Wallace link to, 105, 106

Roosevelt, James: opposes Wallace-ites, 26

Rosenman, Sam, 29, 84, 129 n. 73

Ross, Charles, 11, 20, 110

Ross, Irwin: on Taft-Hartley veto, 25; on State of the Union message, 71; on civil rights plank, 76

Russia. *See* Soviet Union

St. Paul Pioneer Press: reaction to Wallace candidacy, 48

Schapsmeier, Edward L., and Frederick H., 15

Schlesinger, Arthur, Jr.: opposes Progressive party, 96–97, 101

Schmidt, Karl, x, xi

Selective service legislation: Truman calls for, 58; Wallace opposes, 64, 66

Shannon, David A., xi

Snyder, John, 28

Socialist party in 1948, 87

Social security increases: Truman on, 69

South: in Clifford's analysis, 30, 44; press reaction in to Wallace candidacy, 48–49

Soviet Union: Wallace stand on relations with, 2–8, 12, 13, 64, 67, 68, 90; administration's stand on, 20; Clifford's appraisal of policy toward, 31, 36–37, 41; increasing tension between U.S. and, 76–77; Wallace tries to open communications with, 80; Wallace calls on for peace, 93; ADA fears, 94; effect of actions of in Berlin and Czechoslovakia on 1948 campaign, 58–59, 63, 76–77, 99

Spingarn, Stephen J., 83

Stalin, Joseph: Wallace letter to, 80

Starr, Louis E., 21

State of the Union Message: use of as strategy, 42–43, 68–71, 127 n. 32

Steinhardt, Laurence, 59

Stokes, Donald, 108

Straight, Michael, 12, 31, 88, 122 n. 21

Sullivan, Gael, 22–23, 72, 132 n. 37

Taft, Robert, 44

Taft-Hartley Act, repeal of: Wallace favors, 64; talk of Progressive influence in, 86

Taft-Hartley bill: effect of Truman's veto, 14, 23–25, 34, 38, 66

Tax revision: Clifford's recommendations on, 43; Truman on, 70

Taylor, Glen, 54, 62, 65

Tennessee Valley Authority: Truman on, 69

Theoharis, Athan, 107

Thomas, Norman, 87

Thurmond, Strom, 74

Time magazine: on Taft-Hartley veto, 24; on Wallace candidacy, 50; on Isacson election, 54; reports Truman attack on Wallace, 77–78; on Progressives' influence, 111

Tipton, Harold, 128 n. 61

Truman, Harry S.: question of Progressive party influence on, x–xii, 62–63, 80, 86; assumes presidency, 1; Wallace critical of, 2–5, 16–17; break with Wallace, 7–13; keeps Democrats in party, 14, 25; conciliatory to Wallace, 17–20; attacks Wallace, 21, 57–59, 77–78; and Taft-Hartley veto, 23–25; liberal image of, 26, 41, 85–86, 111; strategy to elect, 28–45; recognizes Israel, 36; silent on Wallace, 49–50; Wallace reply to attacks of, 59–60; refuses to debate foreign policy, 63, 76; Wallace attacks, 66; and State of the Union message, 68–71; on civil rights, 72, 75, 76; foreign policy statements of, 79; attacks of on Progressives, 80–85; Humphrey on, 96; no liberal alternative to, 103; endorsements of, 105, 111; and ADA, 105–106, 132 n. 35; victory of, 108; Wallace aids victory of, 109, 110; Catholic vote for, 109; Wallace letter to, 109; the press on victory of, 111; not a liberal victor, 114

Truman Doctrine, 14, 17, 23; Wallace critical of, 17, 25, 58, 67, 99

Tugwell, Rexford Guy, xi, 94–95, 104, 110

Turkey: Truman requests U.S. aid to, 17; Wallace critical of policy toward, 67

Tyler, Gus: on Isacson election, 56

Union for Democratic Action, 88
Union party (Father Coughlin's), 109
United Automobile Workers Union, 63–64
United Nations: Wallace favors building peace through, 64, 68; Progressives criticize use of, 66, 67; Truman pledges support to, 70, 79
USSR. *See* Soviet Union

Vandenberg, Arthur, 7, 10
Vardaman, James K., 29
Vaughan, Philip H., 127 n. 45
Veterans of Foreign Wars, 21
Vinson, Fred, 80, 110

Wagner, Robert F.: on Wallace candidacy, 49–50
Wallace, Henry Agard: impact of, x–xii, 23, 24–25, 35, 62–63, 71, 86, 114; in Roosevelt administration, 2; forms third party, 2, 26, 27; disagrees with Truman foreign policy, 2–10; firing of, 10–11; edits *New Republic*, 11–12, 89; support for, 14; as critic of administration, 15, 16, 25; Truman criticizes, 16–17; Truman does not denounce, 18, 19; Boykin criticizes, 20; Truman attacks, 21–22, 57–58, 77–78; California Democrats disassociated from, 26, 27; Democrat strategy on, 30–33, 39–40, 45, 60–61; ADA against, 40, 90, 93–94, 98–101, 106–107; Democrat research on, 44, 78; announces candidacy, 46, 93; press reaction to, 47–49; Republican reaction to, 49; Democratic reaction to, 49–52, 74–75; test of strength of in New York, 52–56; linked with Communists, 56–57, 60–61, 85, 92; Liberal party attacks, 57; on Czech takeover, 58–59; states his stands, 63–65, 90; Russian actions undermine, 76; letter of to Stalin, 80; Norman Thomas opposes, 87; PCA supports, 90; defines a liberal, 90–91; Tugwell praises, 94–95; Humphrey baits, 96, 107; Loeb criticism, 97, 103; critical of Soviet Union, 102; and Communists in party, 104; McGovern supports, 104; aids Truman victory, 109, 110; letter to Truman, 109; *Time* magazine on, 111; on election, 112; breaks with Progressives, 112–113; domestic platform of, 126 n. 10

Washington Post: reaction to Wallace candidacy, 47–48; criticizes president's attack on Wallace, 59
Wechsler, James, 96
West: Clifford on strategy to win, 40, 43
Whitney, A. F., 23, 25, 103
Wyatt, Wilson: on Wallace candidacy, 46; on Isacson victory, 55; and "Creed for Liberals," 91–92; opposes third party, 92–93; praises ADA anti-Wallace pamphlet, 101

Young, Harold, 31